BADGER VALLEY

Also by Monica Edwards

THE UNSOUGHT FARM
THE CATS OF PUNCHBOWL FARM
THE BADGERS OF PUNCHBOWL FARM
THE VALLEY AND THE FARM

Monica Edwards

Badger Valley

THE QUALITY BOOK CLUB
LONDON: 1977

This edition by arrangement with
Michael Joseph Ltd
© 1976 Monica Edwards
The Quality Book Club
125 Charing Cross Road
London WC2H 0EB

ISBN 0 7181 1488 4

Set and printed in Great Britain by
Tonbridge Printers Ltd, Peach Hall Works, Tonbridge, Kent
in Times eleven on thirteen point on paper supplied by
J. Dickinson & Co. Ltd, and bound by Redwood Burn
at Esher, Surrey

For Jenny
And all her animals, wild and tame,
including F. C. Badger

ILLUSTRATIONS

CHAPTER 1

I think sometimes of how near we came to losing the valley
and going away from it for ever. Few turning points in my
life have left me with a deeper feeling of chill.

At the time there seemed no way of avoiding it. My
husband Bill was fighting for his life after his tractor had
rolled over him, and our twenty-one years of farming had
come to a sudden end. For a time I tried to continue without him, with the help of our son Sean and friends who
came at once, but this arrangement could only be tem-
porary; he and they had lives and work of their own in
distant places.

During the weeks that Bill was in hospital we both came
to realise that the farm would have to go. In defiance of
expert medical opinion he was recovering but, already past
the age when many think of retiring, we knew that he
would not be fit again for the arduous life of farming.

We had been refused permission to build a small house
for ourselves in a corner of the farm orchard, and quite
properly, since the farm is in a scheduled area of out-
standing natural beauty. No other little house offered itself
anywhere in the neighbourhood and we prepared ourselves
to move, perhaps far away, leaving behind everything that
had become dear to us in nearly a third of a lifetime. To
me the dearest thing of all was the wild valley, a ten-acre
woodland of almost magical beauty, with its bright stream
and hidden paths and its wild creatures that no longer
considered me an intruder. Much as I loved the old farmhouse and buildings, the garden we had planted, the
fields of many contours and the Jersey herd which we

had bred ourselves, I knew that I should miss the valley most.

Then, through a incredible and to us, then, unknown intervention, the Council reversed its decision and granted us permission to build. A year had already passed since the accident. Bill was home and gaining strength, but the cattle had gone. We might quite easily have been far away and the farm already sold with all its fields and woodland, but we had been slow to take this final step. Now at least we could stay in our own country and now, surely, after all my despair, the valley could remain our own. The farm could be offered without it. Bill was in agreement about this. Although the valley didn't have for him the enchantment that it had for me he understood how I thought about it. Neither of us supposed that its retention by us would make much difference to the desirability of the farm. This was where we were wrong.

There was of course no purely agricultural value to the wild valley, a place of steep woodland, largely inaccessible except to the walker and the agile walker at that. We were soon to discover that other people besides myself were aware of its charm. By far the best offers we received for the property were conditional on the valley and the whole orchard being included. After some uneasy debate with ourselves and each other we made up our minds. Bill expressed our conclusions: 'Better to stay where we both want to be, and to keep the valley, than to be richer somewhere else.' And so it was.

During the summer that followed, we watched our new house being built in the orchard as we negotiated the sale of the farm. These were strange months, of slowly loosening the ties to the old house and the hilly fields, so that we should not feel too sharply the wrench of letting them go. It was, of course, a wrench all the same. But I remember the evening of the autumn day when we had finally signed away our life there, and how the strongest feeling I had was joy that we had kept the valley.

I was in my usual place under a clump of hazel at the

side of the woodland track, the wood golden now both above me and on the ground – gold even in the air when a breeze brought more leaves falling. Everything seemed to me brighter, more sharply outlined, as things do which have been nearly lost; small sounds, as of a leaf falling, were clearer. It was almost as if I had never properly considered the wood before, and now was dazzled by its reality. I was not alone and seldom was that autumn.

Sitting near me was Frances (Goldie), the young Australian nurse who lived with us. A year ago she had been a stranger, calling at the farmhouse because she had read about it, and now was still with us. There were also to our annoyance two of our four cats, Rover and Haile Selassie. Cats and dogs seldom mix well with wild animals. Every night we tried with devious strategy to give our cats the slip, but often they were more devious than we and joined us part-way through the wood or arrived later at the rendezvous, presumably having trailed us.

We were waiting for the valley badgers, who regularly, came up to the track to see what we had brought for them – usually it was peanuts and raisins – but especially we looked for one half-grown cub, Arwen. When she was very small, in the early summer, she had been found one morning unconscious in a nearby field, and Frances and I had managed to revive her. The story of her recovery and return to her family is told in another book*; in this, I will only say that it was she who began our real adventures with wild badgers, who changed our status from hidden watchers to people who were recognised and accepted by the valley badgers.

Haile and Rover were waiting, too. Rover was not much of a problem; he was closer to the wild than the Abyssinian Haile, and I think may have identified himself more with wild creatures. With his long luxurious coat he was not a cat one would expect to find living rough in a wood-pile, but he had taken up life with us from a really tough hobo existence. Now he sat peacefully washing himself on the

* The Valley and the Farm

dry fallen leaves, just as if we had been in the farmhouse kitchen.

Both cats knew that badgers would soon be on the track, but where Rover accepted this as quite proper and natural, Haile seemed always to be possessed of the idea that we needed protection. This was a great problem to me. We had at last gained the trust of the badgers after years of natural suspicion, and I didn't want them to see me as a bringer of hostile companions. Haile was about a third of the weight of a single badger and was usually several times outnumbered, but still he would rush an approaching party and, incredibly, put them to flight. The mere audacity of his cobra-hissing charge was enough. After a rout of this kind he would come back to me very pleased with himself, waving his puma-tail and stropping-up ostentatiously on a handy willow-trunk.

To Arwen alone he seemed to extend tolerance, as if appreciating that she was in some way special to Frances and me. Usually she came up from the woods before the rest of her family, so that on nights when Haile had followed us we were able to leave before the other badgers arrived, scattering a few peanuts for them to find in the fallen leaves.

I remember this particular evening as the first time we actually spoke to Arwen since, months ago, she had spent two days and a night in the farmhouse. The moon was nearly full, its rays falling in visible swaths through the trees, one spotlighting the end of the path from the woods. Haile had trotted down this path to his usual look-out under a triple birch from where he could see into the valley, and now he came leaping back to sit alertly a few feet away from me. I knew that a badger was approaching.

Arwen came with the slow zig-zag of a badger testing the wind, and paused in the moonbeam like an actress taking her applause. She had always been tiny, the smallest of that year's cubs, but she had a perfection of coat and outline, even of movement, that was not equalled by any of the others. I said, 'Arwen,' and she turned and looked, as if surprised that our species had voices, but she was not discomposed. Arwen was never discomposed. She came on now, her black button eyes very bright and expectant. I held out a hand with nuts and a few bits of cheese on it. Her black muzzle lifted and checked the air again, found all correct, and the next minute was in my palm, cold and wet and snuffly.

I said again, encouraged by success, 'Arwen, pretty badger, Arwen.' There was no pause in the crunching but she glanced up, as one noting a new thing.

Seeing that we were going to be allowed to talk. Frances said softly, 'Haile's coming to you. He's smelt the cheese.'

I tossed a bit for him, afraid of too close a confrontation in case his tolerance should break down, but he wolfed it and came closer. Another bit, and a refill for Arwen from the other pocket, and then – there was no help for it – I had Haile eating from one hand and Arwen from the other.

'Every time we don't bring the camera,' Frances said, 'we regret it.'

Arwen thrust her nose into my duffle-coat pocket but, finding no more scraps, padded across in front of Haile to see what Frances had. This was more than Haile could stand, even from Arwen, and he made a sudden rush at her. Any other of the badgers would have retreated at once, but Arwen swung round with a retaliating rush of her own. For a moment I was horrified, visualising a half-blinded badger and a mortally injured Haile (no other British animal can inflict a bite as terrible as a badger's), and wondering what to do, until Frances and I realised with astonishment that Arwen's whole idea was play. I doubt whether Haile's original idea was playful, but since Arwen had elected to see it so and she was a forceful badger, however small, he may have decided that the best thing was to see it her way.

Our spotlit woodland theatre now presented for us one of the most enchanting entertainments we had ever seen there. Drama we'd had, tragedy even, but slapstick comedy never – I chase you, you chase me, I only fell over because

I was looking backwards – and Rover with one paw still lifted for washing, looking on with a wonderstruck expression.

It was over too quickly, with Arwen's widening circle whisking her off into the dark valley and Haile trotting back to us looking a little sheepish. We didn't wait for fresh characters and a new act. The next night, perhaps, we should succeed in eluding the cats and have all the badgers at our feast.

CHAPTER 2

After that one evening of moonlit play, Haile's attitude towards Arwen hardened to hostility. He may have decided that he had been tempted into too much friendliness and had better stop it altogether before any ground was lost to the enemy. We began to take more devious routes to the valley in the hope of avoiding him, but sometimes even so he would turn up and join us and we would have to leave the woods early. Haile's love of the valley was and is almost a passion. Nearly every morning and in most weathers he would set out across the fields, following us if we were going but alone if we were not.

Rover was still too enchanted with home life after the wood-pile to come with us often, but he would station himself at the top of the farm track to meet us as we returned. I think that he was anxious when we were out of his sight, lest his heaven of domesticity should fall. It was the same if we went out in the car. He would be in the garage on our return, pounding the floor to greet us.

I was sad about the brevity of Haile's truce with Arwen, not only because of our delight in watching them play together but because Arwen alone of the badgers stood her ground and refused to be bullied by him. She would meet his hissing advance with a short rush at him, her fur rising not only down her back but all over her, so that she looked like a ball of grey smoke, and then return to us with a proprietorial air. I was still afraid that, sooner or later, one of them might badly injure the other.

We were at this time gradually moving the accumulation of years from the farmhouse to the new bungalow. Fortunately Haile was fascinated by these trips up the orchard hill with familiar household items and began to spend more time investigating the new territory, especially when cat-flaps were fitted at the back porch and kitchen doors. Although we were still living at the farmhouse, clearly a new den was being prepared. Frances and I had a week of peaceful valley evenings.

It was early November. The woods were a brighter gold on the ground now than over our heads, but more stars flickered through the branches as the leaves fell. The moon had not risen but our six-volt lantern-torch was hanging in its regular ash tree, its beam falling on to the track like a pool of private moonlight, the Badgers' Moon we called it. They had grown used to this, through an initiation of flash-guns and smaller torches. As long as the light was static or moved slowly they took little notice of it. Sometimes they would snap at a moth floating in the beam, as the cats did, too; our very small torches they would tolerate at even a few inches' distance, which was useful when they had roamed behind us out of range of the bright beam.

After a wet October, the woods had dried and were rustly underfoot. We heard Arwen's approach before she came into our sight; invariably she was the first. Small, beautiful, bold and very confiding, she had no fear of us, but once when she caught the scent of a stranger in the valley she rushed back to the sett in a panic. We were glad about this, as it showed that she knew us as individuals and not just as humankind. Although, of course, domestic animals know and differentiate between people, we had never been quite sure that we weren't putting the badgers at the risk of trusting humanity in general.

The eyesight of badgers is poor, but their hearing is very good and their sense of smell really phenomenal. They live in a world of scents impossible for us to imagine, moving fast and freely in a dark world thick with obstacles.

This evening, as Arwen was doing her quick spot-check on our identity (boots and hands O.K., coats passed in-

1. (*Above*) Arwen with Frances

2. (*Right*) Arwen trusted us in a most confiding way

3. The old house – closer than a field's width

4. The new house – it had everything but character

5. Haile Selassie – outrageously arrogant

6. Good, kind Rover

7. The boar taking crusts into the sett

8. A solitary minute fox cub

spection) others of her family, as we could hear but not see, were already out gathering bedding. Arwen paused to listen as the unmistakable raking noise came to us from the dark woods, and I visualised the gatherers as I had often seen them, shuffling fast backwards, always backwards, with their pile of dry leaves and bracken tucked between throat and forelegs. They never made a mistake in direction, never bumped into any obstacle and never looked round to see where they were going.

How do they do it? Some observers claim that scent is the answer here, too, but muzzles are at the front of animals. Close familiarity with the gathering ground has been suggested, but badgers use many different routes for bringing in bedding; some gathering places can be quite a distance from the sett. I have seen bracken raked as far as seventy yards.

Arwen allowed us to scratch the back of her neck as she ate delicately from our hands. Although they have few parasites, badgers often groom each other with a nibbling action as horses do, and we felt our scratching was appreciated.

We always tried to take offerings that were as near as possible to the natural food of badgers, avoiding sweets and white bread and so forth, and not allowing them too much in case the edge was taken off their zest to forage naturally. Arwen always knew when we had more in our pockets, kept for her brothers and sister. This evening she snuffed at our jackets, trotting from me to Frances and back. I put my hand over the pocket-opening but her muzzle pushed under it and she scraped the pocket with her paw. Finally, trampling all over my knee, she burrowed her head right inside my coat to discover if there was an inner way to the pocket before jumping down and trotting back to the valley, her short light tail the last thing we saw in the moonlight.

We waited. Faraway bangs reminded us that it was nearly Guy Fawkes' Night; the strange sadness of church bells drifting up the valley reminded us that it was Sunday

17

evening. The sounds of bed-gathering ceased and the only valley noises were the wind in the trees, the tawny owls calling to each other and the full stream rushing. Then there were four white-striped faces at the edge of the darkness; Arwen had returned with her brothers and sister.

These three were much shyer with us than she was, jumping when we moved even slightly and looking at us with deep suspicion. We had scattered a few more nuts and bits of brown crust after Arwen had left us, and now she led the others on the treasure hunt, their muzzles ploughing easily through the leaf-litter. There would not be one peanut left in fifteen minutes, so acute is their sense of smell.

The shy cubs soon forgot their fears in the excitement of hunt and discovery. They yikkered and scrapped and snapped over each find, fending off rivals with a swinging side-slam as badgers do.

I was not yet much good at recognising individual badgers with any certainty. Arwen I knew and one brother, a rough bruiser whom we had named Bully Boy. The other two I never really did distinguish, and they were the first to leave the valley and go away to make their own lives; after this night I never saw them again. We had read that cubs leave home during their first autumn but I was saddened at the thought that, on any evening, we might see the last of Arwen too. Bully Boy we enjoyed and appreciated for his bouncing toughness, and would be sorry not to see his galumphing approach any more, but as Haile had once seemed to understand, Arwen was special.

The parents of these cubs never accepted us, nor came anywhere near if they knew we were in the wood. Our best views of them were always from the other side of the valley when they were quite unaware of us.

The cubs found and fought over what was probably the last peanut, and sat and scratched for a little before leaping into a whirl of rough play and loud yikkering. For a while we seemed to be forgotten, and sometimes had our welling-tons tripped over in the wild shenanigans.

18

Cub games often go in rings, sometimes plain chasing but I have seen all four gripping each others' tails and swirling in a tight circle. One cub starts the tail-holding – it can't hurt as much as it looks – and quickly the others join in. The ring of cubs doesn't revolve in one place but moves about like a whirlwind until suddenly it breaks and all are scattered. This evening it was plain chasing, faster and faster then, in the manner of all young animals, suddenly they stopped. One hiccupped twice (too soon after eating, my mother would have said) and the four of them nosed for a minute in the leaves just in case something had been missed, but it hadn't. We knew our entertainment was over when four white tails bobbed away out of the torchlight and into the valley.

CHAPTER 3

Now it was not only our belongings going up the hill to the new house, but ourselves as well. The cats had often followed us on our many previous expeditions up the hill and they did so now; Haile and Rover and the older Burmese pair, brown Pardos and tiny blue Hula the hunter. They couldn't have realised that this trip was final, this time there would be no turning round and going back down the hill. To us, it was a strange and unreal experience. Home – the home we had known for so many years – was closer than a field's width but as far removed now as another century. It had seen many centuries. No one knew its building date, but it was there in 1332. Sturdy and beautiful in stone and oak and two-inch brick, with its sweep of cat-slide roof, its protecting oak and yew trees, the honeysuckles on its walls, I knew it like an old coat. Now it was empty, no light in its windows for the first time since we had begun to live in it.

No house could have been more different than the one we now went into; so new it could hardly help being brash, but it did its best. Warm, light, airy, convenient, with glorious views, it had everything except character. We called it Cowdray Cross, after the field next to it. The old farmhouse furniture looked surprisingly at home in it; the long kitchen especially seemed our sort of kitchen when we had brought in the big scrubbed table round which so many uproarious meals had been eaten, the wheelback chairs and the dresser with its blue and white plates. There was even an Aga, as in the old days, but a new one, oil-fired and unfamiliarly blue.

We never got used to the marvel of the skies. In the farmhouse, deep in its own valley, we never saw sweeps of sky and not much sun. People used to come running down from high Yew Tree field in the evenings shouting, 'Come up the track and see the sunset!' Now, on our hill looking over the farmhouse roof we could soak up all the sun, see all the sunsets and the moon as well. I would often gaze from the windows over the fields in moonlight, looking for deer, a fox or a badger. Photographing sunsets became a new excitement. On the way home in late afternoon and seeing a tremendous one brewing, we would say to each other, 'We must get home in time to catch this one!'

It was a little further to walk to the valley, but Rover and Haile were with us again whenever we failed to outwit or outrun them. Passing the dark farmhouse they would sometimes go in through the cat-flap that was still in the old kitchen door, only to rush out again banging the flap behind them, not liking the blank cold and emptiness which they had never known in that place before. Eventually builders would be there, altering this and installing that, but not yet, not for a long time yet.

Now that the leaves had fallen it was much lighter in the night woods, and we could follow the paths without torches. Once again, after the months of leaf-canopy, we could look up through branches and see the stars, sometimes the moon, and clouds flying over.

Bully Boy also had now gone away, perhaps following the nameless cubs to whatever unknown place and life had drawn them from the valley. Only Arwen still came to us, indeed often was waiting for us. Plump and sleek for the winter, as is proper for badgers in autumn, there was nothing about her to remind us of the tiny chilled waif we had carried home in early June.

Usually we had the cameras on those November evenings, with two flash-guns tied on to the hazel trees. These didn't worry her at all; she was a most self-assured badger, one might almost say complacent. Even with Haile hissing at her from behind any handy tree – he knew better than

21

to try more with her – she was perfectly composed. Sometimes she would give him what one is tempted to call a disdainful look, calmly eating from our hands. Haile never came to eat from the other hand again, but waited until Arwen had gone before leaping across to see what we had saved for him.

Rover was generally little noticed by the badgers, peacefully washing himself at the edge of the torchlight pool and, for his part, they had probably been a familiar feature of the night woods and fields in the time when he roamed his lonely way hunting his supper.

Arwen was curious about everything unfamiliar to her world, and there was naturally much that wasn't badger-like about Frances and me. Frances has fair and very curly hair. She was wearing it short at that time and, with the torch behind, it looked like a shining halo. Arwen would reach up her delicate muzzle to investigate this mystery. A ring on my finger fascinated her and she would nibble it gently, so that in the end I left it at home. Buttons and zips were interesting, as were the toggles on our duffle-coats. Wellingtons were dark holes to be snuffed down inquiringly, especially if a peanut had fallen into one, and coats could sometimes be dived into if not firmly belted.

She trusted us in a most confiding way, allowing herself to be rubbed and scratched and stroked quite freely. Through her I learned much about the physical nature of badgers; the roughness and shading of the coat (each hair on the back and flanks triple-banded, light-dark-light, to give an all-over greyish look), the roundness of the small teddy-bear ears, whose elfin-pointed look comes only from the backward tufting of the white hair at the rims, the short legs and long, strong digging claws that would hold my hand down as her lips softly picked peanuts from it. I knew well the dished sweep of her striped face with the black bright boot-button eyes so untypical of a night-living animal.

It has been argued, on the evidence of their small eyes and ears, that badgers are not truly nocturnal animals but have become so only through ages of persecution. Some badgers born and reared in captivity are reported as having become diurnal.

On December 2nd, my notebook says, we took Arwen some scraps of old honeycomb in a screw-topped jar, from which we decanted it into a saucer. She enjoyed this greatly and then tried to make off with the jar. I had to push it down inside my coat and tighten up the belt.

This was the last we ever saw of Arwen.

December 3rd, my diary says, 'Waited until 8.40. No badgers.'

December 5th and 6th: 'Arwen did not come.'

December 13th: 'Impossibility, it seems, of maintaining contact with Arwen. Many watches during last two weeks. Nothing. But one night – full moon, valley floodlit – I heard swans' wings going over. Fox quickly and silently passed along track.'

December 20th: 'Have not seen Arwen or any badger for a long time, though have waited most evenings at the usual place.'

We now began to watch from the other side of the stream, directing the torch-beam across the valley to where the great ramparts of the ancestral sett jut from the hill about sixty feet away. I had cut sitting-places in the hill opposite the sett, with foot-places below them. The hill rose steeply behind forming back rests, so that the ledges were like comfortable chairs in which we sat on rubber garder-kneelers. We had learned how to keep warm in winter woods, with ski socks and fleece-lined gloves and extra pullovers and hooded coats. When there was a moon the valley was breath-takingly beautiful, the tall trees coming down, down from the high land to the bright stream that rose in the Devil's Punch Bowl.

There was little to see at the main sett, with all its five entrances and the paths that radiated from them. In the short nights of summer, badgers are forced to come out before darkness in order to have enough time for foraging. One can expect to see them within a few minutes of the same time night after night. But in the long darkness of winter they please themselves and get up when they feel like it, or not at all if the weather is particularly bad. They have put on plenty of fat for just this purpose, and can afford to live on it for a few nights without discomfort. That they do so is plain from the slim lines they present in early spring.

Frances and I spent many blank hours on the ledges, and when we did see a badger it was just the sow or boar or both coming out and quickly slipping away along one or other of their habitual paths. Once there were three, but all we could say about the third one was that it was not Arwen.

We knew, now, that Arwen was not in the valley. New cubs were doubtless expected in late winter, and the yearlings had vacated in their favour. It is natural for young birds and animals to do this, we knew. Still we didn't know how it happened. Did the young leave of their own accord, from some deep instinct of the order of things or from a spirit of adventure and independence, or did the elders drive them away? We didn't know, but one day I was to see for myself and learn.

As the winter settled in, Rover gave up coming with us and preferred the warm Aga in the kitchen, but Haile, who was a sort of Spirit of the Valley, came often. It didn't matter now, as we sat on the ledges with no badgers near, and he skirmished in the woods with joyful abandon as if all that land belonged to him.

In January the snow was nearly six inches deep. Our friends Nic and Natalka brought their skis and we sailed about the hilly fields; at least Natalka did. My granddaughter Lindsey was staying with us then; she was twelve at the time. She and Frances and I were novices at the ski game and floundered and lurched about with hopeless hilarity, enjoying ourselves greatly, making mini ski-jumps for ourselves over snowy hummocks. There was never anything like this in Australia, Frances said, unless you were in the Snowy Mountains.

24

When we weren't ski-ing, we trudged about the fields and woods and lanes looking for animal tracks, the snow sometimes over our wellington tops. Snow gives quite unequalled chances to see which animals are going where, and sometimes why: the pounce of a fox landing in a flurry of feather-marks; roe deer stepping to the glade and scraping for grass there; a most beautiful double wing-print etched in the snow where a pheasant had taken off; and most interesting to us, the tracks of the valley badgers.

Anyone who imagines that British badgers hibernate should visit their territory after snowfall. From hole to hole of the main sett their broad five-toed spoor led us, slithering precariously along their paths that clung to the valley-sides and up through the hazel copse to the dung-pits. These are usually within seventy yards or so of the sett, sometimes much closer, and are always scrupulously used by badgers. They are a useful guide as to whether a sett is occupied and sometimes as to what the residents have been eating. Worms form a great bulk of the badger's diet and of course show no obvious residue in dung, but often one can find beetle wing cases, rabbit fur and teeth, and in their seasons blackberries, hazel nuts and acorns. The dung is not covered by the badgers but quickly disappears under drifting leaf-litter.

From the dung-pits the badgers had forged out through the snowy fields, calling in at a small single-hole sett in the hedge of Barn field on their way to further holes used by them on Upper Highfield Farm, where Arwen had been found. The snow must have been chest-high to the badgers; their trail was a deep furrow ploughing through it. Sometimes on steep places they had clearly tobogganed, leaving a trail as smooth as an otter-slide. I hope they had fun! Otters surely do, climbing up to the top of their slides again and again, to have another go.

I took some photographs, but in great stupidity elected to try out a red filter which I had been given for Christmas, 'to cut the dazzle'. I could at least have used it for only half the exposures, one might have thought, but when I

25

am silly I am silly on a grand scale, it seems, and I used it for all. Red filters with black and white film make blue skies look dark, and snow reflects the blue of the sky. My immaculate snowfall came out looking like a week-old fall in the Black Country.

February 5th is marked with a red line in my notebook. It was not marked at the time, but months later, when I remembered it as the beginning of a new stage in my affairs with the valley badgers.

I was alone on the ledges that night. Although Frances still often came, the valley did not have the same enchantment for her now that Arwen was gone, and I was on my own just as often that winter. Frances had in any case never been as obsessed as I was with woodlands in the night. There was enough light from a three-quarter moon to see without a torch and I sat at ease, marvelling at the dramatic light-show. The sharp contrasts of moonlight and the sheer spectacle of the effects always surprise me. I thought of the care and planning and expense that go to make our human light-shows, and how this great performance is tossed off by the moon as routine, and for no expectant audience at all.

A soft purring-whickering sound drew my attention to the main sett opposite. Three badgers had come out of the north entrance and were playing together in the way one sees usually only among cubs or when cubs are present, except that it wasn't ordinary play. They were excited, snuffing and gently nibbling each other. One of the three, a sow – perhaps Arwen's mother? – was the main source of interest, but all made the loud purring noise continually for about three minutes. This is an affectionate sound, made by parents to young cubs or in the breeding season by an adult to its mate; in all my watching I have never heard it except at these times.

The sow who was the cause of the excitement hurried down into the sett again, the others sitting in the moonlight for a minute or two before they followed her. February is not the breeding season, nor is it a time of much excitement among badgers, but it is the month when most badger cubs are born. Could all the excitement and scenting, the hurrying back underground, mean that cubs had just arrived? I thought that this was probably the answer, and something of the badgers' exhilaration touched me, too. It would be around two months before I could expect to see them, but the thought that probably they were born was enough to please me greatly.

CHAPTER 4

On February 9th two of the badgers were digging and bed-gathering. The third came out presently and dunged in a hollow between the north and south entrances before hurrying in again. Only in really awful weather or, in the case of sows, when cubs are too young to be left for long, do badgers dung as close as this to their setts. I was more certain about the presence of a new family.

Old bedding was dragged out with earth and sand, and sometimes stones which tumbled noisily over the rampart edge of the stream below. New bedding went in, crisp and rustling. There is, as far as I can see, no foundation at all for the theory that badgers bring their bedding out to air, presumably taking it in again later. All the bedding I have seen outside – and that is quite a lot – has been jumbled up with earth as it was raked out, and is left to lie there, adding to the great terraces outside the sett entrances. Only fresh new bedding has ever gone in when I have been watching.

I wondered about the third badger, another sow. Did the boar have two mates? Or was she a kind of single aunt helping around, as elephants are said to have? Before the end of the month she was gone, and I saw only the mated pair. Usually, after a few minutes together grooming one another outside the entrance the sow would return to the sett and the boar leave on his own. The digging and bed-gathering went on almost nightly when the weather was dry.

We are told badgers do not take food into their setts. With the valley badgers at least this is not true. One day early in March I left pieces of stale brown bread near the main sett and in the evening was watching from the ledges opposite. The moon was nearly full and the night milder after a very cold week. The boar came out at 8.30 (it was the winter when we kept Summer Time) and padded along the rampart to where the crusts were. Although twice in the previous year I had seen food taken in, I was surprised to see him pick up a crust and return with it to the north entrance, and even more surprised when he turned round and went down the hole backwards, holding his head high as if carrying something large like a rabbit. He was out again in a minute and took in a second piece, again backwards and with the same exaggerated head-carriage. It was rather comic– such a small crust – and I found myself smiling. Another minute and he was out again, but something in Valley field above the sett startled him and he dived underground.

I waited a while, listening to the tawny owls' beautiful question and answer, before calling up Haile and turning for home; the steep woodland path, the silent fields, a light in the porch with Rover faithfully waiting under it for me, and music in the house.

'I'm certain there are cubs,' I said to Frances. 'The old man was hunting crusts for them!'

Two days later the sow took crusts into the sett. First she sampled a piece for herself and then took in five pieces, all *front*wards, before beginning on bed-gathering. This evening she was collecting dry grass in very large bundles. Grass is easier to handle than leaves, and big heaps are often brought in. One pile slipped out of her hold and began to roll down the bank, but skilfully she caught it back and trundled it inside.

On my way home, as I crossed the stream, a small trout showed in the torchlight before darting under overhanging roots. The stream is too shallow for anything sizeable but now and again a fingerling makes its way up, incredibly negotiating a five-foot vertical waterfall on the way – or, if not, how does it reach the wild valley?

Each day now I left a few small bits of bread at the sett, and each evening had the fun of seeing them taken inside. The sow had two systems: either she gathered them all at one go, as a puffin gathers fish, and carried them in, her mouth bristling with fragments, in which case she stayed down about twenty minutes; or she took them one at a time, staying down for an average of three minutes. She always went forwards with either system.

The boar, when he did take pieces inside, continued to reverse head-high into the hole.

I had further fun trying to get this entertainment on to film, and sometimes I succeeded, especially when Frances was with me to help by directing the lantern-torch on to the badgers while I focused the camera with the 400 mm lens. We were using the tele-flash made especially for me by my son Sean, and we were also uprating the black and white film to as much as 16,00 ASA and developing it accordingly.

The badgers were completely used to our torch and flash by now and took little notice, but we were always careful that our scent did not reach them and also to make as little noise as possible.

One evening at the end of March I had a surprise from a different woodland animal, a roe buck, normally shy and retiring where people are concerned. It was a very cold and starry night and I was on the ledges with my camera. The buck came along the stream path below me uttering his short harsh bark as he stepped delicately over fallen branches. I looked down at him and he lifted his head and looked up at me. I was wondering if I had time to refocus for a photograph when suddenly the buck came pounding up the nearly precipitous valley-side to where I was sitting. He stopped only one yard away and stared at me and the camera; the velvet on his horns was sharply visible. I wondered for a moment if he might decide to charge me – a captive roe buck could and might kill a man trapped in a cage with it, but nearly all animals in the wild prefer evasion.

True to his wild ways he swung away and plunged on up the valley-side to stand at the top looking into the chestnut copse – I could see him against the stars and dark branches – then through the fence with the agility I had often admired and away out of my sight. This was the only time in my life when a deer of any kind has appeared to challenge me before racing away.

When we were into April I knew that on any evening we might see the badger cubs. April 8th was the earliest date and May 3rd the latest in my notes for first sightings. Besides the anticipation of this thrilling annual event, there was also all the glory and marvel of spring moving into an English wood. Although the winds remained cold and easterly, wood anemones began to star the valley. The woodcock were back, their strange churr-squeak passing above my head as they flew up and down the valley at dusk. I would stare through the still bare branches and sometimes catch a glimpse of the quick dark form against the sky.

Everything was very dry. Bed-gathering continued, and mostly it was old grass going in.

The badger pair still took in crusts whenever I provided them, but now were only staying underground for about one minute each time: probably the cubs were growing more ravenous and coming nearer to the entrance. Once, later in the evening, a fox came trotting along the high path to the rampart and snuffled around there, scratching for crumbs, but few were left and it quickly glided away. The badgers sniffed where the fox had been before they padded away up the valley, and again my hopes of seeing the cubs were disappointed. I left with the moon just coming over the hill.

Haile Selassie gave Frances and me a shock one evening by suddenly appearing from inside the lower hole of the main sett. He was so much smaller than any of the badgers that I was always in fear for him; his behaviour was often quite outrageous one would think, from a badger's point of view. Only the same afternoon, when Frances and I

31

were repairing valley fences, he had disappeared down the north hole and stayed for some minutes, long enough to worry us, before emerging from that same lower hole.

We had a way of calling-up cats in the valley by 'squeaking' through our lips – a mouselike noise known to everybody – so as not to disturb any wild creatures, and now we squeaked-up Haile. He came at once, crossing the stream by the 'badgers' bridge', an old fallen tree, and joined us on the ledges where he was a nuisance as always when we had the camera, pushing against the carefully adjusted tripod and generally skirmishing and bouncing around.

This evening a neighbour friend was also watching from the bank above us, and all the time he was there Haile growled at him. I thought of the two Burmese peacefully stretched out by the Aga at home, and good kind Rover keeping faith at the place where he usually met us, and wished that Haile could occupy himself a little more on those lines. But of course we loved his tough independence and wild woodland ways, and didn't really want him tamed too much.

April was cold and the spring late.

On the 21st, Frances saw a very young fox cub at an earth in the part of the valley called Inner Wood. The next day we both went along and saw three cubs there, blue-eyed, dark and fluffy. They were squabbling over a dead rabbit. At this age, fox cubs don't really look like foxes any more than young chicks look like hens. They were enchanting to watch, both fierce and babyish at the same time, with chubby faces and short fluffy tails. There was no sign of the vixen.

That night the cold weather incredibly turned suddenly much colder. For three days we were not able to go to the valley at all because of rain, snow and frost.

There was no sign of the fox cubs on the following two days, nor of any kill outside the Inner Wood earth; but on the second of those days I had the first glimpse of the badger cubs. Watching on the ledges with Haile I saw the boar go away from the south hole, which had not been used much in the winter. Five minutes later the sow appeared at the same hole, and I could see cubs' heads behind her in the entrance. It was 8.30, Summer Time, twilight, and I was using my 7 x 50 field glasses which pick out details in light too poor for me to see even shapes without them.

As I watched enthralled the boar returned carrying a smallish prey, I supposed a young rabbit, and took it into the hole brushing the cubs back in front of him, the sow following. A strong musk smell came across to me; badgers musk when very excited or afraid. He went away soon after this, and the sow nosed round for my crusts and raisins, taking a few bits in to the cubs before coming right down to the stream. This was unusual; I have seldom seen badgers drink. Almost always, perhaps after digging and bed-gathering or play, they move off straight away without going down to the stream at all.

She crossed the running water, chest-high, as if it didn't exist and without drinking. On my sides he immediately picked up my scent and began following it, her muzzle to the ground. This was interesting. One would expect a badger to rush away from human scent, and I have often seen them do so. Did she associate mine with the food scraps that had been carried in my pocket?

She came on, steadily climbing the steps that I had dug into the valley-side and stood at the ash tree by the top step, looking at me for some time. Haile, luckily, had gone off into the chestnut copse. When finally the sow had satisfied her curiosity and gone back across the stream, it was dark and very cold. I scrambled down the steps as quietly as I could and along the stream path, squeaking-up Haile as I went but without any success. Climbing up to the oak tree glade I shouted for him but the woods were silent except for tawny owls calling down the valley.

Frances met me near the empty farmhouse; she had become uneasy because it was so late. She said Haile was at home and had demanded supper.

Listening to the late news we heard that this had been the coldest April since records began.

On the 29th, after an hour of entertainment from a family of baby squirrels, a pair of roe and the tawnies who were feeding young in a hollow oak by the stream, Frances and I were rewarded. It was nearly dark but our glasses picked out the badger pair at the north hole. They were very cautious, going in and out for a while; then suddenly there erupted a pile of quite big cubs, at least three, perhaps four, bigger than any first-timers I had seen before. I took one photograph with the long lens and electronic flash, whereupon there was a loud growl-bark and the whole family dived into the sett. The adults had been well used to the camera and flash for a long time, but probably they were alert now to the slightest risk to the cubs. We left, climbing in the dark down the dug-out steps with the camera and equipment while the family was still underground.

CHAPTER 5

On the last day of April – still very cold – our watching at the fox earth rewarded us, if one can call it that. A solitary minute cub came wobbling to the entrance and stood there for a minute peering from eyes half-closed with discharge. The dark woolly coat was scruffy and unkempt. A dead cub lay in the undergrowth near the hole and there was no kill outside.

As we watched, the scruffy cub lifted its head and uttered a small cry so desolate that my heart ached. Clearly some disaster had happened to the vixen; at least one cub had died and probably we were looking at the last survivor of the family. Days of unequalled cold and wet weather, with the loss of the mother, had been too much for tiny cubs to withstand.

A few more minutes of watching convinced us. We went softly out of the wood and ran home. Here, luckily, there was chicken ready for roasting. We took the raw giblets and some diluted milk (for without its mother's milk the cub would be dehydrated) and hurried back to the valley. We were not sure as we crept towards the earth if the cub would let us get near him, but his sight was poor because of the infection and his good sense of smell was bombarded by the life-saving giblets held out to him. I put them down with the dish of milk and withdrew. The cub devoured them ravenously and then tottered to the milk. He was about twelve inches from nose to tail-tip, leaves were stuck in the fur of his coat and he looked weak and unsteady.

When he had filled himself up and gone back into the earth we picked up the dead cub to bury it and went home, leaving the remainder of the milk.

The next morning we took some mince and duck broth, and the orphan cleared up most of it. We debated the idea of taking him home to try to rear him in safety, but turned this plan down almost as soon as we had thought of it. The idea of a bungalow fox didn't appeal to either of us. Both of us felt, as we had done about Arwen, that to a wild animal freedom is all; better death than captivity. We decided to try the almost impossible thing, to rear him in his own earth. We would be novice vixens, bringing him food and drink until he could find his own. We would have a go at his infected eyes, too, said Frances the trained nurse – if we could get hold of him.

Generally we like to think of names for the animals we watch; it is easier when talking about them and making notes. We called the fox-cub Toddy, from an old English word for fox – Tod; and so we were launched on a wholly fascinating and time-consuming job.

It was May now, and we were seeing the badger cubs nearly every evening from the ledges. I was worried about Haile and wished he would stay away from this part of the valley while the cubs were small enough to arouse fierce protective feelings in the parents.

The tawny owls solved this problem for us – literally at a stroke and just at the right time. They had fierce protective feelings all right, with two very vocal young in the nest and a hunting cat in their territory. For a couple of evenings they simply watched him as he prowled about in the wood, but there came a moment when he was too near their tree. Both the owls immediately swooped on him, screeching. Taken by surprise Haile crouched at the stream-side fearing to move; the owls had dived so close that I thought they might have hurt him. He mewed to me, but as I was hurrying down from the ledges to rescue him the owls swooped again. This time, on their upflight, he streaked across the badgers' tree-bridge and vanished into the hazel copse towards home as the owls sailed off triumphantly downstream.

36

This frightening experience made a great impression on Haile, and for the rest of that summer he kept to the Inner Wood end of the valley, away from the owls and badgers. Our worries about his relations with the badgers were over for a while, but soon we found that they were to be transferred to the orphan Toddy.

A day or two after the owl attack we went to the earth with the usual diluted milk and a leg from a rabbit caught by Hula. We found Haile at the earth. There was no sign of Toddy but Haile looked quite innocent of any slaughter. All the same, I was anxious for so tiny a cub and decided to take Haile home while Frances waited at the earth with the milk and rabbit.

I heard my first chiff-chaff on the way back through the fields. Spring, however late, was surely coming although oaks, ashes and elms were still only in bud and I had seen but one swallow. There was a little heat in the sun at last, and when I got back Toddy was out enjoying it, in a little nest he had made by curling up for warmth in whatever sunshine there was. He was tearing at the rabbit leg, his minute Christmas-tree tail stuck out stiffly so that we could see a smear of dung under it; he had no vixen now to clean him up. Still, we thought he looked a lot better. Now that he was filled up with food and drink twice daily he no longer had the sunken look that had caused us concern. Even his eyes seemed better, or at least no worse, and because we were uneasy about causing him panic by needless handling we decided to wait a day or two to see if they would heal by themselves.

Hula, the great hunter (her record was seventy-two rabbits in one season) let us down the next morning. Usually she could be counted on to bring in at least one rabbit by breakfast time, most of which she left for the other cats until we began snatching it for Toddy. So this day we tried him on tinned cats'-meat, served on a burdock leaf to look more natural. The milk of course was as usual in a non-tip dish of dark colour.

The cub approved of the cats'-meat, but while he was

still eating it Haile glided out of the shadows. I began to see a logical reason for his interest in the fox earth. Still, he did not push in and try to take the meat, but sat waiting with the carefully averted gaze that cats assume when trying to conceal their motive. I was so glad to see that his motive appeared to be attacking Toddy's dinner rather than Toddy himself that I gave him a little from the tin in my pocket, on a burdock leaf of his own. He was used to the idea that all cats had their own dishes at home, and seemed to accept that one leaf was his and one Toddy's.

We fed the fox cub again before we set off for the ledges in the evening, walking through fields golden with buttercups. The boar was already out on the rampart eating crusts and raisins when we came up the stream path at five past eight. He saw us and went in but not hurriedly, then peeped out from the lower hole and watched us settle. In ten minutes he was eating bread again and took several bits in to the cubs. We were amused to notice that he had abandoned his backwards entry which, for all I know, shows that male badgers don't mind learning a useful thing from their females.

At five past nine the whole family emerged, the four cubs very big and bouncy. We took several photographs without any reactions from the badgers, and this evening the boar stayed with his family, sitting on the rampart and letting the cubs jump about roughly all around and over him, sometimes even worrying his ears and pouncing on his tail.

Meanwhile, the tawny owls sailed by silently hunting for their noisy owlets, and they and we and the badgers for once had no worries about Haile.

On May 5th the fox cub had one eye sealed. We decided not to wait any longer but to try first-aid treatment. On our second visit to the earth we took, as well as a bank vole which I had cut open and the usual milk, a small bottle of saline solution and a tube of eye ointment containing neomycin. Toddy was used to my sitting in the rough grass near him when he was eating, and as long as

I kept still and quiet he didn't mind my being barely an arm's reach away.

He was lapping the milk, with snuffles and sneezes, when I put out a slow hand and closed it gently round him. Whatever the little waif lacked it wasn't spirit; he growled and the needles of his teeth immediately pricked hard, but not hard enough to pierce my skin. There seemed no weight to him; he felt like a bundle of soft fluff but his tummy was nicely round and full. I held him with one hand under his chest and muzzle and the other round his middle so that he couldn't bite again, while Frances bathed his eyes with the professional skill one expected of her. When they were clean and dried she put in the ointment, and then we tidied up his coat a bit – no good being vixens however novice if we couldn't clean up a cub – and finally we set him down outside his earth and watched him rush inside.

'There was a time when he couldn't rush like that,' Frances said.

We went so far as to begin planning how we would later teach him to hunt, that is if Haile and stray dogs and all the perils of the wild would allow him to grow up safely.

The next day Rover – who seldom hunted now – brought in a field mouse; just what we wanted for Toddy if we couldn't have rabbit. There followed a series of snatches beginning with my grabbing the mouse from Rover – regrettably, but I felt the cub had more need of it; Rover's once scraggy figure was now pretty circular. Toddy snatched it at once from me and I snatched him and Frances did his eyes again. They were better but not quite cured. As soon as I put him down he grabbed the mouse again and trotted into his earth with it. We left his usual watered milk and some cats'-meat with extra vitamins and minerals.

Hula caught a rabbit just after her lunch. She still managed to eat a fair part of it before I got the rest for Toddy. The cub pounced and dragged it into his earth. A good amount of his milk was gone and most of the tinned meat.

39

We began to feel like quite experienced vixens; but the problem of a regular fresh food supply had to be tackled. The cub needed raw carcasses with fur or feathers and guts complete; these provided essential roughage and vitamins. We couldn't absolutely depend on Hula.

We thought about day-old cockerels, often discarded by commercial hatcheries. We could store a dozen or two in the freezer part of the fridge. I telephoned a hatchery I knew of and they said we could have as many as we liked if we collected them. We did this, and stored them in our mini-morgue, two or three to a small plastic bag, except for a couple needed in the morning.

Over the next few days Toddy lived alternatively on chicks and rabbit. For some reason he was suddenly much more wild and elusive. He would peer out of the earth at us as we put down our offering and wait until we had withdrawn before darting out to snatch the carcass and vanish down the hole with it. Milk always disappeared but we no longer saw him lapping. He was always too quick for me to catch him again for further eye treatment. We wondered if he had had a fright. Haile was often in that part of the wood when we arrived and, although we were now fairly sure that he was not likely to attack the cub, we remembered his hostile swearings at the badgers and thought he could have been putting on a terrorist act. In some ways it was a good thing, we thought, because our worst fear for Toddy was that he might be unwary enough to fall victim to some roaming predator, whether human or otherwise. He had no mother to teach him caution, and this was something we could hardly do for him.

One morning I did at last manage to capture Toddy again, by crouching above the earth and catching him as he came out, so that Frances was able to dress his eyes a third time. Hula had been splendidly efficient, providing fresh-killed rabbit, and we took some photographs of our now sleek and lovely fox cub carrying his luncheon home.

On the ledges in the lengthening evenings we had great entertainment from both the badgers and the owlets. One owlet was much more adventurous than the other and took to what one can only call climbing. It would come out of the nest-hole towards dusk and start ascending the oak tree. Too young to fly it used its claws like crampons, and sometimes its beak as a kind of ice axe, flapping its wings in tight places. We never saw it descend but both owlets were always in the nest when we arrived.

Spring was really with us now, as well it should have been in the middle of May, the trees so bright and delicate a green that one could scarcely believe it and full of song birds, too, so that waiting on the ledges was like sitting at a concert where the orchestra played only for us. Cuckoos were calling, but so few. Where, oh where are all the cuckoos of my youth, the nightingales of our early years at the farm? I have not heard a nightingale for more than eight years.

CHAPTER 6

The badger cubs were growing obstreperous, always trying to burst out like new wine before their parents thought it late enough in the evening. At first the elders simply ushered them back in, as sheep-dogs with a restless flock, but soon tougher discipline was needed. The boar began to opt out of the situation and mooch off when the nightly insubordination began, but the sow was more determined. Failing to herd them into safety in the ordinary way, she would lose patience and start dragging them one at a time by the scruffs of their necks. But now broke out an old trouble applying also to hens and cows and often experienced by Bill and me in our farming days: as soon as you turn your attention for a few minutes to another escaper the first ones break out again. And, of course, there were several entrance holes to this sett, a point that the cubs quickly used to their advantage.

This sow must have been a tremendous disciplinarian really, especially once her family was properly underground. When finally she had got them all into the sett again – not without twenty minutes or so of rough treatment to establish the balance of power – the battle was over for the evening. She would stay below with her cubs for a few minutes (what doing? More heavy rule or just settling them cosily with a last swig of milk?) before calmly emerging and padding away. There would not be another sign or squeak from the cubs.

Both owlets were flying now, and the wild cherry was in bloom and pools of primroses lay in the woods. The last half of May began warm and sunny with warblers singing.

Frances and I were working at the fencing along the west boundary of the valley, content with our lives and our surroundings, saddened by only one thing. Toddy was not at the fox earth. After a day or two of not seeing his snub little muzzle looking inquiringly from the hole, and of finding our offerings untouched after each visit, we knew that he was not there, or if there, not alive. He had been in such splendid condition, alert and lively, his eyes and coat better, and he had grown quite a lot. It was unlikely that he could have died except violently.

We began to search the length of the valley, not an easy matter with so many old thickets and so much undergrowth surging. The whole of spring was burgeoning now after the cold weeks, and the hedges foamed with may blossom.

It was a week before we found our cub, or what was left of him. He was not in the valley at all but in a farm field about eighty yards from his earth. As we had said, he had no mother to teach him caution with the world, and this was one service we could not have done for him. We buried him in the woods where we had buried his brother. It was the end of an episode: no good being sad about it, but we were. We had so nearly succeeded.

At the ledges, the badger family continued to interest and delight us. The sow had begun to relax her control over the cubs, as I dare say she saw was inevitable, so big and rough they were growing. The boar seemed to like them better the rougher they got and would play rushing tumbling games with them, pausing for intervals of gentleness when he would hunt by the stream and return with some minute offering – a slug or a beetle? – to feed them like a row of baby birds in the entrance to the sett.

Quite early on we saw that the boar had a favourite cub. We thought it was a little sow. Usually she was with him, and often before the others had emerged. Sometimes he would even let her accompany him when finally he went off foraging, although the sow generally went alone leaving the other three cubs racketing around the sett. I see that many of my valley notes made at that time begin: 'Boar

43

and his favourite cub went away towards Valley field. Few minutes later sow and the other three cubs emerged.'

In June Frances took up her nursing career again, as now that we were settled in the new house there was not enough for her to do. She was with us on her days off, but usually I was alone in the valley, even Haile still keeping his distance after the affair of the tawny owls.

I decided to move my watching place from the ledges to the old track, where we had waited for Arwen in the autumn. The cubs and their parents often went up there, and I wanted to be closer. Now that the cubs were so big and strong I thought that the adults would be less likely to rush them underground on detecting me, but at first I was careful to sit down-wind of where I expected the family to come up from the sett in the deeper part of the valley. After scattering a few peanuts and raisins in the leaf-litter on the broad track I concealed my silhouette as best I could against an ash tree and waited. There was no need for a torch, of course, on these long summer evenings; the badgers were out in full daylight, sometimes even in sunshine.

In a few minutes the boar came up the path from the valley with, surprisingly, all the cubs trailing behind him. He led them on to the track and paused and looked towards me – how much could he see, I wondered? – then turned and slowly retired to the valley, leaving the cubs on the track.

The nuts and raisins were discovered by the young ones at once, and squabbled over with excited yikkering and side-slamming. They were still rootling around when, a few minutes later, their mother came padding up the path. She called to them with a noise I have never heard before or since; not the usual purr-whicker but a sort of zizzing grass-hopperish noise. Either this was a really serious warning, not to be ignored by the most unruly cubs, or they had simply exhausted the treasure-hunt; whatever it was, they trooped meekly after her back to the valley.

The next evening when I was in the same place, the

boar came up alone. The proceedings were rather strange; I have never before felt so acutely under observation as I did then. For about fifteen minutes he watched me continuously, first from one vantage point and then from another, usually behind some log or tree which gave him a little cover. Now and again he would lower his head to eat a scrap, but he appeared to be watching me still all the time. Finally he left the track and went off down the path towards the valley, but at the triple birch where the path dips out of sight he turned and looked back before moving silently into the trees.

After two days of ceaseless rain I went again to the track in the valley a little before nine o'clock and waited, as eager as any watcher of a thriller serial to see what might happen next. At nine the boar appeared by the triple birch and stood there looking at me. He was a big fellow and somehow looked bigger, even majestic, standing at the rim of the valley quietly surveying the area which he had so carefully inspected before the rain. I sat still, not looking directly at him, for I think that animals are sensitive of being stared at. He turned to go, stopped and looked back once over his shoulder, then silently vanished. Badgers seem big clumsy animals, often pounding noisily about the woods, but even huge ones like the cubs' father can move like shadows.

Presently he returned, this time with the favourite cub. They nosed out nuts together for a few minutes and then went away towards Valley field. They had hardly gone from my sight when the other three cubs came skirmishing up from the valley, the sow trotting after. The cubs were clearly remembering their previous finds on the track and whirled into the hunt with joyful yelps, ramming each other like boats in a battle. Often they came within inches of my feet, quite regardless in the excitement and competition of discovery. For a while their mother hovered between the track and the birch tree, watching in a puzzled or doubtful way it seemed to me, perhaps hoping that they would come with her back to the familiar safety of the deep valley.

45

But the cubs stayed on. Until after dark they rollicked and rootled and groomed and played and fought, and I might not have been there at all for all the notice that they took.

I was so intoxicated with the magic of these woodland antics that I sought out Bill to tell him when I got home. Rover had met me at the garden gate and we went together into the garage which was shared between the car and Bill's workshop. He had set up a lathe and brought in logs of apple and cherry and maple, and he was making most elegant little wooden dishes and bowls. It seemed a fitting place to talk about the mysteries of my kind of woods, leaning against his bench in the scents, beauties and mysteries of his kind of woods, and watching the bowls being shaped by his skill.

Frances had two days off from the hospital and I picked her up the next afternoon. We went over to the valley early, lingering many times on this rare fine evening to admire the wild roses ramping in the hedges, the honeysuckle swags waving from trees and scenting whole areas, a patch of bird's nest orchid, strange and yellow under the beeches, and drifts of germander speedwell like sky fallen down.

This was the evening when the pattern for the summer watches was established. The boar had decided on a policy, and from now on followed it almost without variation until the cubs grew too big to need his protection. We seldom saw the sow again from the track watching place, but each evening the boar would come up from the valley with his favourite cub close behind him and the other three in a roistering gang a little further back. The old man would stop where his path joined the track and let the cubs push past him to scrabble and sniff for the scraps we had scattered. Sometimes he would root out for himself the odd nut that had fallen beyond the edge of the track, but most of his time, for perhaps ten to fifteen minutes, was spent on sentry patrol. From tree to tree he padded on his round of inspection, stopping at each one to stand and watch for a while before moving on to the next. Always I had that

46

strange feeling of being under surveillance, on trial as a suitable creature to be trusted, and I did my best to give satisfaction, sitting quietly and certainly never hob-nobbing with his children when he was watching.

After a while he would be satisfied with the situation and would trot away on his nightly foraging. The cubs by this time were usually quite near to me, snuffing out the last of the bits, and it was easy to get them to eat out of my hands. As the weeks passed they grew tamer still, looking on me it seemed as some kind of harmless wood-land feature that had peanuts in its pockets. They would trample all over those parts of me that were accessible, boots, legs, lap, hands or arms. Only one of the four was too shy and for a long time stayed too shy to allow strok-ing, coat-ruffling, scratching and such liberties. Because of this I called her Shy, and by her ragged-edged face-blaze I could recognize her easily. This one I was pretty certain was a female; she had the narrow head with delicate jaw-line and the bushy tail which are typical of sows.

Now that I was beginning to 'get my eye in' over the matter of identifying individuals I found it easier and com-pletely fascinating. No two were alike. This is as true of all other animals as it is of people; I remembered a shepherd I had known in my youth on Romney Marsh telling me how he knew every sheep by sight in his flock of three hundred. But it does take practice before one begins really to see wild animals as individuals.

Two more of this year's cubs were fairly easy, and I had little doubt that they were male and female. The male – broad face, strong shoulders and thin tail usual in boars – was a perfectly delightful animal, self-confident and bold but very gentle. I called him Proudfoot after a hole-dwelling hobbit in *The Lord of the Rings*. He was recog-nisable by a very broad face-blaze, but I knew him too by his bulk and his winning behaviour. The other sow-cub was 'Daddy's Favourite', and often she was not with the others on the track, presumably for this reason. I called her Puff because she had a permanently fluffed-up little tail,

47

like an old-fashioned swan's-down powder puff.

The fourth cub mystified me so much as to sex and character that 'it' didn't get a name at all that summer, but I thought that it was probably a male.

My own favourites were Puff and Proudfoot, who were each other's favourites, too; they were usually close together and came and went in company. Often I had these two eating from my hands at the same time, while Shy kept her yard or two of distance and Nameless would stand boldly on my feet or cower behind a tree according to the mood of the moment.

The cubs were often astonishingly clumsy, considering how sure-footed older badgers are. They would trip over fallen branches or each other, and once Puff fell off a log on to her back! They were usually precise and gentle when eating from the hand; no grabbing and gobbling but each nut or raisin picked up very carefully. Once I did have a finger mistakenly but gently taken by Proudfoot; it was immediately released and my palm licked.

Sometimes their half-playful fighting was funny to watch. They would roll and fall about in yelping heaps, short legs stuck up in the air, and chase each other in mad whirling rushes about the woods. A cub agressively approached by another would sometimes put on a kind of porcupine act, *all* the back and side fur being quickly raised like porcupine quills, making the cub look enormous, then lowering as quickly and returning to normal sleekness.

Puff once, very playful, staged a fight with a foxglove, boxing at it for several minutes before swirling after her own tail in a very tight circle.

On all these summer nights the father of the family kept his vigil, watching from different places until he had assured himself that all was well. He never came close with the cubs but I think in some obscure way approved of their associating with me. I knew that probably the whole answer was in my being a provider of tasty morsels, but still I didn't understand why he kept his own distance and took so little for himself. Now and again, after leaving the cubs with me,

9. Suddenly a pile of cubs erupted

10. Mad whirling rushes

11. Proudfoot was the first to allow stroking

12. The author photographing the badger cubs

13. Jack, with the champagne bottle stripe

14. Roly after peanuts

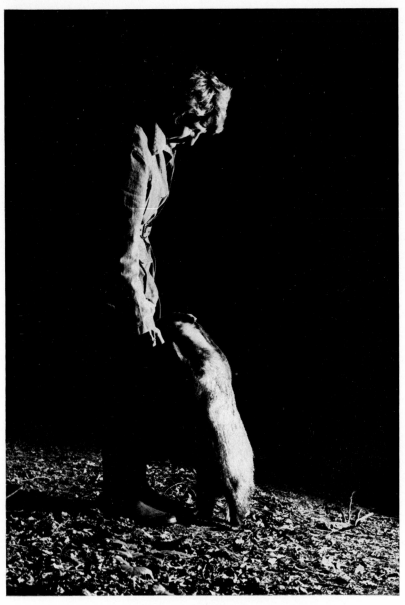

15. Roly ate from my hands as I stood

he would return after an hour or so and lead them away through the hazel copse into Valley field, a favourite foraging ground. Once or twice I saw the sow, a shadowy elusive form among the tree trunks, waiting for them to join her.

Haile I knew was often in the northerly part of the wood, his respect for the tawny owls still sharp in his mind. He would come mewing his greeting and leaping through the trees to join me as I walked home, his white throat in fawn body-colour showing up as dusk flowed into the valley.

CHAPTER 7

There was no question of retirement for Bill; he disregarded incidentals such as accidents and growing older. His activities at the new house multiplied; the wooden bowls were scarcely a beginning, being overtaken fast by contouring our rough site for lawns and laying down a concrete terrace and path right round the house. The terrace began its existence as a strip a mere four feet wide, and then was interrupted for a long time for the starting of a kitchen garden. Meals in the garden that summer saw us sitting on this narrow strip in a straight row, like people at a theatre, passing dishes and conversation up and down the line as our toes hung over the raked earth: but the view across the folded fields and woods was quite perfect.

One would have thought this might be enough for Bill to have on hand, but all was overtaken by a surge in what for many years had been basic bee-keeping. His half-dozen or so hives were quickly increased to eighteen. This was achieved by leaving his name with the police as a man willing and able to collect unwanted swarms. Since his accident I had been the sole driver, and was likely to remain so as his sight and hearing were affected, so I now found myself liable to be called out with Bill any evening to some urgent, even despairing call. 'They're in the bathroom; we daren't go in. Please come quickly!' 'They've swarmed in the chimney; could you possibly come at once?' 'It's the bicycle shed; we can't get at the children's bikes.'

Not having much empathy with bees myself – or they with me – I spent much waiting time in the car that summer, reading, doing crosswords, chatting up people's cats, wondering if the badgers were looking for me; then the drive home, the back of the car humming with sheeted menace and Bill in his element having everything precisely under control.

I was glad to be back in the valley and for a time away from the crises of human activity.

Soon Frances would be leaving to spend the English winter with her parents in the Australian summer. 'I'll get three summers in succession,' she told me, 'because I'll be back in the spring.'

Meanwhile she had a stretch of free time and was with me more often in the evenings. She was entranced with the cubs and with their father's careful vigilance from his watching places in the woods. She wanted to know if I ever talked to the cubs, as we used to do with Arwen, and I said no, because of never being sure where the boar was and what he would make of it. One evening, when we had seen him trot away up the track with his favourite cub, I whispered to Nameless what a beautiful cub he was. All three cubs whipped round to stare at me and bolted away into the valley.

Frances thought it might have been the whispering – too much like Haile's hissing – that they had objected to. So the next night I tried again and said my piece clearly. The cubs took no notice at all, except to glance at me casually as they went on rooting out nuts.

Proudfoot came to eat from my hand; he was careful now about not taking my fingers. His easy nature made him lazy; sometimes he would lie flat on his front with his back legs spread out when he was eating. He had been the first of these cubs to allow stroking or touching in any way. All the cubs would hold down my hand with a restraining paw, so that I couldn't draw it away until the last nut had gone.

One evening early in August a single cub, the nameless one, came up the valley path, but it was accompanied by a fox cub. This really was surprising and interesting, as the valley badgers seem always to have objected to foxes

51

near their sett. I recalled the fights I had seen and written about earlier, and was sad that I was unlikely ever to see cubs of the two species playing together, as I had heard about from other places. These two, although ignoring each other, seemed content to be together, both amicably searching for scraps, until suddenly the fox cub got my scent and bolted.

Scent is an interesting subject about which little is known, so unimportant is it to the lives of human kind. We enjoy some scents and dislike others, but we don't, indeed can't, use scent very much as information about places and events. It is difficult to imagine ourselves into the lives of animals for whom scent is of primary importance. Most wild animals dread and flee from the scent of man generally, except animals in remote and lonely places where he is still a stranger with his weapons, traps and poisons. But although man has a general specific smell, as do horses, dogs and so on, each of us has a particular variation of this smell, as much our own as our fingerprints. Dogs have no trouble in identifying an individual by scent alone, even simply on a piece of clothing. I have noticed, though, that all dogs like to get very close to the person or thing being smelt. Dogs will approach warily and sniff one's hand or clothes within an inch, or even touch with the muzzle, before satisfying themselves completely about identity. Cows will do the same.

Badgers also like to get pretty close even to a trusted person for scent recognition. At about six yards they have typed the scent enough to come closer, but they will make further checks until the final one with muzzle nearly touching. Even at this stage, if Frances or I chanced to be wearing something different, they would be uneasy for a while, double-checking other items about us until fully satisfied.

It was rather like getting a thing in focus visually, I thought. We might glance along a lane and see a vaguely familiar person approaching, but he is out of focus and we are not sure until he comes nearer. I would imagine my scent being 'out of focus' to the badgers – mixed and

52

confused with other scents, perhaps – until they were close enough to receive it clearly. I was glad to discover how individual to badgers the scents of people are, as I had worried about endangering the valley badgers by accustoming them to human scent. I knew now that it was only my scent, and to some extent Frances's, to which they were growing accustomed. There was no doubt about this, as several times when I had taken friends – making sure that they could not be seen, were down-wind and could be relied upon to be quiet – the wind had veered and the badgers immediately departed.

The badgers' scent was of course perfectly clear to me, as I should think to anybody with a reasonable aural sensitivity. Slightly akin to that of foxes but pleasanter, less acrid and more musky, I knew it well. There was always a faint aroma of it about the badgers, but they would often squat, pressing their anal musk glands against the ground or a tree root to mark their territory, and then the scent was very noticeable. Sometimes if suddenly startled they would emit musk as they rushed off, leaving the scent hanging in the air.

My scenting-range, as one might call it, is far shorter than that of badgers. I can pick up their scent at about sixty feet on a favourable breeze if they have just musked, but they can detect a human being at two hundred yards with the lightest wind movement.

Towards the end of August Frances left for her Australian visit, and my watches were usually solitary. The cubs' father began to slacken his nightly vigil and often did not come up to the track with them at all, but they grew bolder and bolder, excepting always the one called Shy. If anything she grew shyer.

Haile was back in the southern part of the valley again, having got over his fright with the tawny owls, and once more I was bothered by his swearing at and chasing the four cubs. If it had not been for Haile, I should have thought the badgers were the kings of the woods. When ground was disputed with foxes, the badgers always won. A dog that challenges a badger can get a terrible reception. Once in this August a roe buck was grazing on the track, coming slowly towards me, when the boar badger appeared through the trees. The roe looked at him and at once trotted off in my direction (so I knew I was not the cause of his departure).

One evening in September this same roe buck came grazing down the track just as two of the cubs appeared. He glanced round to look at them, but this time continued grazing. When the cubs saw him, it was they who retreated; perhaps because they were only juveniles, not carrying much weight in the world of roe bucks? The buck did not see me and the wind was right; he passed closely and disappeared through the woods towards the stream.

By the end of September the cubs would come out of the valley when I called them. Sometimes they would be at the edge of the wood waiting for me if I was a little late and would trot along close by me if I did not have Haile with me. I have also been escorted as far as the oak tree glade on my way home.

In October there was much digging and bed-gathering for the winter. The cubs, now nearly as big as their parents, were working too, if a little fecklessly. Like young things of any species they would tire of the dull job quickly and rush off to play, leaving heaps of bedding lying in the path to the sett; or if they were digging they would leave raked-out litter in the entrance instead of scraping it neatly away. Badgers dig out their setts in a most distinctive way, not scattering the earth as most digging animals do but raking it always along the same narrow path from the hole. They often continue vigorously scraping right to the edge of the rampart leaving a deep groove, easily recognisable as badgers' work.

The scene as the badgers worked and played in moonlight was most beautiful, the wild creatures moving through the black and silver woods, free and splendid and going about their natural affairs. Sometimes one would pause for a few minutes beside me and sit for a friendly minute or two, just as if we were badgers together and I not a member of the human race, for centuries their most deadly enemy.

These cubs of course had known me since they were tiny; to them I can only have been a natural thing of the woods. There was no established fear and distrust of our species in them for me to try to overcome. If there had been, I should without much doubt have failed, as I failed with their parents and with all other mature wild animals whose trust I had tried to gain.

It is so easy to win the confidence of very young badgers; all one needs is patience, quietness and some basic under-standing of badger nature. In my case, I didn't even need patience; the whole venture was so enthralling to me that no patience whatever was called for, at any time. The woods themselves, even without the badgers, have always been magical enough to hold me in thrall. It is not the trust of cubs that is hard to achieve. The art is in keeping that trust up to and through the first winter, and beyond if by good fortune they do not leave one's area. This means never losing touch for more than a few days, whatever the rain or snow or frost and whatever other delightful things one might be doing. I do completely understand the viewpoint that the reward simply isn't worth the cost, but it isn't my viewpoint.

In this autumn of the Puff, Proudfoot, Shy and Name-less cubs, no one could have complained about the weather. 'Still Indian Summer,' say my notes for November 2nd. 'Full moon. Cubs ate from my hands in a most confiding way. Puff *lay down* beside me, with paws on my knee, as I found nuts in my pocket for her, and I scratched her shoulder and stroked her. Cubs looked beautiful in moon-light, as did all the valley and woods and fields.'

These cubs were never really at ease if I got up and moved about, although sitting in my place beside the track I could get away with almost anything, such as messing about with my camera, throwing peanuts, blowing my nose (quietly) or even coughing. Sometimes, if they were already at the rendezvous when I arrived, they would scuttle behind a fallen log across the track and peep at me over the top of it – four striped faces in a row – while I set up my camera or hung my torch in the ash tree. Only when I was safely settled on my rubber pad would they approach to see what I had brought.

The Indian Summer slowly faded with the month, its beauty falling with the golden leaves. The last entry for November reads, 'Frost, bitterly cold. Full moon. Two cubs from the birch tree, beautiful in moonlight. Except for cold it was an enchanting evening of crackly frost and moon and badgers.'

This triple birch, on their path from the valley, has a little hollow place where the three trunks part near the base. After rain this is always full of water, a miniature woodland pool, and the badgers often paused to drink at it, although I seldom saw them drink at the stream.

As in the year before, towards the middle of December the cubs, one by one, ceased to come to our meeting place. The last was Puff, 'very appealing, lying with her weight across my knee, eating from my hand and allowing herself to be well stroked and talked to.'

The next night no badgers came at all.

On the 20th, after I had waited for one hour, suddenly in the starlight I saw the big boar at the birch tree. He had come up silently from the valley and now stood there motionless, looking at me steadily for perhaps two minutes, before turning to vanish once more in the darkness of the woods. Was he perhaps trying to tell me that the cubs had gone, I wondered? That I would not see them any more?

I waited another hour or so and then turned towards home.

CHAPTER 8

Now began a long blank period such as I remembered so well from the year before. Day after day my diary says, 'Saw nothing.' 'Saw, heard and smelt nothing.' 'Nothing; no owls, even.' I resigned myself to what I now accepted as the inevitable loss of all cubs as the time approached for the birth of new ones. But still I went down to the valley; it was a magnet to me whatever life it held or lost and in any kind of weather.

I was glad that I did this. On January 20th I was late at the track because of making a detour to shake off Haile. As I approached, I saw in the light from a sickle moon a badger near my sitting place, the first for one month. It ran up into the hazel copse as I came to my place.

The wood was frosty, the slip of a moon winking beyond the swaying branches. I put down my offerings of cheese scraps and brown bread and waited. In fifteen minutes two badgers came to me, one from the copse behind me and the other up the usual path from the valley. I was very excited. So cubs – yearlings now – could come back, after they had gone away from the family sett; and these two were my favourites, Puff and Proudfoot. They came up to me as if they had never been away, eating from my hands and letting me stroke and talk to them, exactly as they had always done.

I feared that Haile might appear, but he did not. Some sudden noise sent the cubs flying after twenty minutes or so, and I called them to come back, but only Puff returned. She finished some raisins I had kept for a special treat and then trotted after her brother. (Walking in the valley next morning I found one undigested raisin in the dung-pit!)

The next night both the yearlings came up from the valley, and also the old boar, who took up his watchful stance by the triple birch as he had done so often before. My diary says, 'They all looked glorious in moonlight, much whiter and more ghostly than usual. Stars very bright.'

What had happened? Had the cubs left on a voluntary journey, in search of new territories, perhaps, and tired of it? Or had they been driven away and come home hoping for a new deal and a welcome? If so, they appeared to have found it; but one could never say with badgers. And where were Shy and the nameless cub?

For the next month Puff and Proudfoot came nearly every evening, but never again with the boar in attendance. They were a continual enchantment. There was the time when, the picnic finished, Puff rolled over on to her back and combed her chest for a long time with her strong blunt claws, her short tail curled to her belly; the time when they didn't think I smelt quite right – I had been with Natalka's Anatolian sheepdogs – and huffed and whuffed at my trousers, but eventually overlooked the matter; the night of rough weather when the wind in the trees was like a storm at sea, the cubs' fur ruffled and the moon flashing in and out of the racing clouds – very dramatic, like search-lights sweeping the woods.

We had snow in late January and I wrote, 'Hungry yearlings ate everything I had. They looked superb coming through the snow; very dark, too, against the whiteness, even with the clouded full moon, whereas in the dry moon-lit woods they had looked so pale.'

A further delight, in that February, was a woodmouse who lived under a tree stump across the track and often came out to eat crumbs and peanuts. Longtailed and fairy-like, whisking so fast that it looked like a brown leaf blow-ing, it would come very close to my feet, I think not properly 'seeing' my comparatively huge but motionless figure. It had no trouble in seeing the badgers and would

58

vanish immediately if a striped face showed on the birch tree path. Badgers, of course, have no objection to a tasty mouse if they can catch one.

Late in the month I saw the boar again. The yearlings were already with me when slowly his big form came out of the darkness by the birch. Proudfoot, standing on my knee, suddenly became aware of him and turned to glance briefly before dashing away through the copse. Could this mean that new cubs were born and the boar was renewing his hostility because of them? Puff, at my feet – always Daddy's favourite – took no notice and her sire glided back into the shadows.

Late that month there was much digging at the main sett and, surprisingly, green grass going in for bedding. Puff and Proudfoot were not using the central part of this ancient ramification, but an outer – though still connected – 'wing' known to us as the tree stump hole. We knew that there was a connecting gallery because we had often seen individuals go in at one end and emerge from the other. Two new dung-pits appeared a few yards above this entrance, and I found in them a few peanut fragments among the beetle elytra, clear evidence of the yearlings.

It was about this time that a third yearling came back, smaller and thinner and hungrier than Puff and Proudfoot. I dropped as much of my scraps as I could in its direction, but this youngster was nervous, coming quite close but 'freezing' when I moved, sniffing my boots but jumping back as it did so. It was, I now knew, the timid little sow that I had named Shy: the fourth, nameless, yearling had in any case a centre stripe much narrower above the eyes. So thin was Shy, compared to the bouncing Puff and Proudfoot, that she appeared to be much longer in the leg. It was strange to see, as she began to flourish and put on weight, how her legs seemed to grow shorter. She had obviously had a hard time on her travels.

So now, with new cubs almost certainly born in the main sett, three yearlings had come home, in contradiction to all my reading and previous observation. Often I was to find things like this happening, against my earlier conception of normal badger behaviour, so that I came to think that there is no normal badger behaviour – just as perhaps there is no normal human behaviour. Do yearlings leave home and stay away? They may do so. Do badgers tolerate foxes? Some badgers do. Do they take food or other things into the sett? Sometimes they do.

Presently I should be asking, are badgers monogamous? Do yearlings ever help to rear new cubs? When cubs leave home, have they been driven away? and other fascinating questions, none with an absolute answer, it would seem, applying to all badgers.

In early April, when Frances came back from Australia, the three yearlings were still coming nearly every evening to the track, but Shy was as shy as ever. I had been away in Italy and had not yet seen the new cubs, but on April 15th Frances watched from the ledges across the stream and saw four, with at least four adults. The new cubs came out at 8.45 and were allowed to stay out for ten minutes before being taken back underground.

Two nights later I saw them for the first time myself. For a week or two the parents were very cautious, ushering the cubs back in before they had been out for many minutes. I too was watching from across the stream, the only place where there was a view of the whole main sett area. At my track sitting place I would not have been able to see the cubs while they were small enough to be playing only in their immediate backyard, so to speak.

After a few days I began leaving honey on exposed tree roots for the cubs to lick. They enjoyed this, and took no notice as Frances and I photographed them with the long lens and flash from the ledges. A very bold cub one evening must have travelled along the length of the underground gallery to the tree stump hole some seventy yards further up the valley, where we saw him emerge. He looked around in a surprised way and toddled fast along the path back to the main rampart where he scuttled in at the north hole. Looking back with hindsight at this incident, Frances and I were certain that this cub was the one that we later named Jack, the boldest, baddest, most undisciplined badger cub we had ever known. Soon we came to recognise his face; he had – perhaps appropriately – a centre stripe shaped just like a champagne bottle (this shape of stripe, we whimsically came to think, was probably typical of bold, bad badgers, for in the following year the roughest cub of the lot also had the same distinctive marking).

A day or two later we went through the woods to repair the boundary fence opposite the main sett, and on the way left some honey at the rampart. It was 4.15 and the sun was shining. We had hardly crossed the stream when Frances, looking back, noticed an audacious cub already out and eating honey. It was Jack. That evening we saw from the ledges a vixen licking those same honey branches.

The new cubs were now occasionally following their parents or the yearlings up towards the track, so I went to sit there again in the hope of seeing them closer. Frances, on the ledges, watched to see what would happen. No badgers came up to the track while I was there; all that I saw was a roe buck nibbling elder leaves and a wood-mouse whisking about a tree stump. When we compared notes afterwards, Frances said that the badgers came out several times and snuffed the air, but went in again every time. The wind was in the north, straight from my sitting place to the sett, so that they must have received my scent clearly. This was a further indication that my idea may have been correct; human scent at a distance of, say, sixty yards, is probably to a badger just general human scent. The distance must be shorter to be recognised as that of a known individual.

On April 26th there was a full moon and I was again sitting at the side of the track. It was now three weeks since I had been in close touch with the yearlings, so that I was delighted to see Proudfoot coming up the path towards me. He was a little wary at first, making several checks on my identity, but soon was champing down bread scraps from around my feet. Then suddenly he found a bigger piece. He looked at it for a moment, then picked it up carefully and trotted off with it towards the sett, holding it very high in the way we had often seen the old boar carry pieces to his cubs. ('How about *that* for Big Brother?' I said to Frances, telling her about it later; I felt sure he was taking it to the cubs.)

In a few minutes Proudfoot returned, accompanied by Puff and Shy and, to my surprise, the old boar himself. This gentleman tentatively munched a few scraps before beginning his old ritual of keeping watch from various standpoints, while Puff and Proudfoot guzzled nuts and raisins and even Shy was less shy than before. After his usual fashion the old boar glided off into the copse when he was satisfied that all was in order, and then came the last surprise of an enthralling night. Out of the woods suddenly came the fourth yearling, the nameless one, whom I had not seen now for over five months. The entry in my notebook is underlined, and after it I wrote, 'Must name this nameless one. Who came back after long travels? Ulysses!'

With his broad face and skimpy tail typical of boars I was sure he was a male, but it can be difficult to sex badgers under two years old. In any event, for the purposes of my records he was now Ulysses.

For half an hour I had all four yearlings close around me. Puff and Proudfoot were soon eating from my hands, just as if there had never been three blank weeks. I stroked them both and they raked my boots aside in their old confidential manner and nosed into my pockets, and Proudfoot sat beside me and groomed himself companionably. I could easily have marked him with the sheep-marker crayon I had brought in my inner pocket (in case, after long absence, I might fail to recognise one of them) but I did not do so because of the two shy yearlings nearby.

I know that I remembered that night in February – more than a year ago and marked in red in my notes – when I was sure that I was present in the valley at the birth of these four who were to become so well known to me.

It was still daylight, the moon just rising through the high branches. The thrush who usually sang 'Wait for me!' was trying a new song that went, 'There it goes again!' (We had once had a very boring thrush which sang 'Dirtie Gertie!' all day long.) Jackdaws were nesting in the hollow oak just north of the main sett. The wood was flecked with primroses like fallen moonlight and I knew that violets were there, although I could not see them. I was perfectly content. 'Think I will not go to Malta,' I see my diary says, concluding the entry for the day.

CHAPTER 9

It was the following evening and I was alone on the track. To my surprise, half an hour before any other badger – 8.15 – Ulysses came up to the triple birch. He saw me move my head and retreated, but soon was back and came up the path on to the track where he had a real feast all to himself. He seemed less wary than his sister Shy usually was and came close to my boots for scraps and for honey in a saucer, but he would not be tempted by raisins in my hand.

He went away towards Valley field and soon Puff and Proudfoot came up by the birch tree and straight to my knee as usual. I tried out the sheep-marker on both the grey and white areas of Puff's coat, but it made no mark at all that I could see. There must be something about a badger's shiny rough coat that resists a crayon suitable for wool.

Still the new cubs did not come up to the track, so I watched from the ledges the following night and saw all four, playing with their mother and Shy and Puff and Proudfoot; there was much rushing in the dry leaves. Ulysses was there too, but not playing. He had five months of hard living to make up and was earnestly foraging for the peanuts I had left around the rampart. I saw through my field glasses that he had scratch marks on his face, and wondered if it was not only hunger that made him stay apart from the family he had left so many weeks ago. I felt, as I had often done, that so much of the life of this family was inevitably unknown to me. What happened when they were underground during the day, or out of my sight in the dark countryside? Were they hostile to the returned wanderer? Were the old pair really content to have the yearlings back, now that new cubs were present? I remembered the total disappearance and non-return of last year's growing cubs – even the gentle Arwen – and wondered.

The next evening I was at the track watching place again and, as before, Ulysses was the first arrival at my feast. After a few minutes of guzzling he picked up a piece of bread and trotted back to the sett with it. Was he, too, feeding the new cubs? When he returned a few minutes later the old boar followed him up the path and as usual watched me carefully from four or five different places. I felt, as always at these times, very much under surveillance. Ulysses took a second crust back to the sett and, the old boar moving off, my stage was empty as darkness began to fall. Then three of the yearlings came up, all except Shy. I peered into the dusk for her and saw her white stripes near the birch tree, coming closer. To my suprise and delight, two tiny cubs were with her, one very bouncy. Their coats – the pale grey of infant cubs – were fluffed out with excitement, making them look like downy balls.

My delight did not last long, for Ulysses turned and addressed the cubs with a strange and hostile noise the like of which I have never heard before or since; a continuous moaning groan, with another sound that was like a porcupine rattling its quills. This rattling had a sinister quality and completely mystified me. How did he make it? Was he chattering his teeth? Or what?

The baby cubs and Shy rushed back to the sett, as well they might. The combination of sounds was fairly horrifying. When the cubs and Shy had gone Ulysses turned the noise on to the other two yearlings, who mooched off behind me in a subdued manner, and I wondered if I would find myself in the middle of a fight; but presently these two melted away into the dark. Ulysses continued his noise for a while and I began to think that he might be ill, or having a fit, but suddenly he stopped and turned round and trotted smartly down the track northwards. He had been only a couple of yards from me.

My diary of these events comments, 'Now I must consider whether to stop feeding the badgers for a while, in case Ulysses attacks the new cubs. It is a pity to lose touch with Puff and Proudfoot of whom I am very fond, but I think I must, in the hope that Ulysses now goes away.'

For a fortnight after this disturbing evening I watched only from the ledges across the stream. It was sad to see Puff and Proudfoot, and even Shy, looking for me at my old track sitting place, and I longed to run down to the stream and call to them. Ulysses remained at the sett, keeping himself to himself, not playing with the cubs as the other yearlings did, but mercifully not threatening them, either.

I occupied myself with watching and photographing fox cubs in Inner Wood and over on Upper Highfield Farm, and a roe doe with a fawn in Valley field. The tawny owls had young again in their old hollow oak south of the main sett. I think that the sound of them stirred uneasy memories in Haile, for he began dropping behind as I came near to that part of the valley, and would wait for me in Inner Wood where he was fascinated by the little foxes. These were at Toddy's earth, and seeing them there stirred memories in me, too, of the little orphan we had so nearly succeeded in rearing to independent foxhood.

On May 19th I risked sitting at the track again. Ulysses was the first one up from the valley, at 8.45, foraging around me more boldly than usual. In half an hour Puff came up accompanied by one little cub, and then Shy with two more cubs. The fourth cub trailed along a minute later. I watched Ulysses anxiously but he seemed to take no notice of the cubs, and I relaxed and allowed myself to enjoy their scrambles around me as they hunted for raisins. They were fearless of me because their older brothers and sisters showed no fear and they took their cue from them. This is how all wild animals learn what to fear and what to accept: but probably there is still some deep horror of human scent instinctive in badgers, for when their muzzles actually touched my boots the cubs exhibited momentary panic.

I need not have worried this time about the returned traveller. My diary says, 'Ulysses seems to have had a change of heart; he was very gentle with the cubs, even allowing them to side-slam him over a disputed peanut. Twice he made the kind of purring noise that is a little like a pony whickering, to one of them. I was not able to leave until nearly 10 p.m. when the badgers had finally gone. Tawnies and woodcock calling.'

The next night I wrote, 'All eight, cubs and yearlings, close around me. Marvellous sight. Only the parents lacking. Cubs less fearful now when their muzzles touch me.' There was, I noted, much side-slamming among the cubs, who also often slammed the yearlings. The patience of even the gentle Puff was a bit strained once and she snapped at a pushful cub, but it was nothing like the Ulysses affair of a couple of weeks before.

The arrangement of yearlings in charge of cubs went on much the same through the last half of May, but never all the eight together again when I was there; the yearlings seemed to share out the nursery duties among themselves. Once Proudfoot alone was left in charge and brought up all the four cubs by himself, shepherding them carefully in a quite touching way. So yearlings do indeed sometimes help to look after the younger generation. This was another question answered, though not conclusively and for all badgers. There seemed to me to be a good reason for this shift of responsibility, which appeared to be total while it lasted, for I no longer saw either parent during this time. Could it not be a way of helping the sow to wean her cubs? Her milk would dry up in a week or two of absence, and I was interested to see whether she would return after a short and probably much needed holiday!

May went out very cold as it had remained all through, and as indeed the springs had been for several years past.

67

More than nine weeks of cold weather, up to date,' I wrote. 'Some ash trees still not in leaf.' But somehow June came in with its usual heady smell of hawthorns and a flush of late bluebells. The cubs were growing bigger and bolder and I was beginning to know them as individuals and to think of names for them. Jack, of course, with the champagne bottle blaze, had acquired his name early, and he never lost his reputation of being the audacious one. He tried once to jump on to my knee when Proudfoot was standing on it and got firmly pushed off by Big Brother. He would stand behind me with his front paws on my shoulder and peer over, and once or twice he grabbed the edge of my jacket in his teeth and tried to pull me away, perhaps thinking of me as a useful food-hoard which he fancied keeping to himself.

Of the other three cubs, one – a little sow, I was sure – had a somewhat similar blaze to Jack's, though less flamboyantly bottle-shaped, and she herself was smaller, slighter and much less dashing. I called her Jess. The third cub, probably a male, had a blaze broad in the middle, in the shape of a candle flame. Frances named this one Piglet. The fourth cub, another female we thought, I called Roly; she had a straight-sided blaze. As it turned out she was well-named, since she developed an engaging way of grooming herself while lying on her back, but we didn't know this at the naming time. She, of all this year's cubs, became the most friendly and confiding, as Jack was the roughest, Jess the most beautiful and timid, and Piglet – when it came to photography or tape recording – the most obliging. I could usually get him doing what I wanted and in the right place, even drinking at the stream, which I had never seen any of the cubs do before the evening when I wanted to photograph this and called him down on purpose.

Only Roly of this litter had anything of the friendliness of Puff and Proudfoot, really enjoying a little petting. The other three were impatient of such liberties on my part, concentrating only on such offerings as I had brought for them and whisking off to play as soon as they knew these were finished.

Early in June, I began to sit in a new place, much closer to the sett itself. I called this the beech tree place, because of the really splendid forest tree beside it: about thirty feet from the ancestral sett and ten from beech tree hole on my left, there were yet two more outer entrances to my other side, so that I was sitting in the middle of the orchestra, so to speak.

The only entrances I could not see were the south hole at the main sett and three further up the valley, the middle, tree-stump and stream holes. The first two of these I knew were connected underground with the main sett, but I had yet to find out what connections, if any, there were between the other four holes of this large complex. This I hoped to do in time by gradually sitting closer to the main entrances, if the residents would allow it.

I could of course see all the entrances at once from the ledges, but at that distance – sixty feet or so – it was more difficult to identify individuals accurately; and this I had to do, to make sure that the animal going in at one entrance was the same who came out from another.

On this first evening I was at the beech tree place soon after eight. Almost at once the badgers began emerging; first the mother and Jack from the main sett (so the old sow had come back), both clearly surprised at seeing me so near. The sow retired at once but Jack came up to me. Perhaps his zestful champing alerted the other cubs for quite soon they all three emerged from the beech tree hole itself – very close – accompanied by Proudfoot. Their astonishment at discovering me almost on their doorstep was quite funny. Even the sight of Jack with his paws on my knee, guzzling, did not reassure them at once, and they gazed for some minutes before deciding it was safe to come nearer. Next from the main sett appeared the mother again and Ulysses. She hastened up the valley obviously disapproving and wishing to have nothing to do with the follies of the young, but Ulysses came up and joined the party.

It was most interesting seeing these six badgers playing around on their own terraces and going in and out of the various entrances, once they had completely accepted my presence there. I could enjoy, too, a whole wide stretch of this beautiful woodland valley with its bright stream and tumbling ferns and honeysuckle swags, instead of the more restricted view up on the track. I could watch the owlets in their hollow tree, and the woodcock roding above the stream, a bird I could usually only hear when I was on the track.

After more than an hour of these delights, Ulysses finally mooched off and Proudfoot led the cubs away towards the hazel copse. Now nearly midsummer, it was still daylight. I went home, contented as humankind can be, through woods full of the scent of holly blossom.

CHAPTER 10

The new sitting place at the beech tree greatly widened my scope in watching this family of badgers, as it did in watching anything that happened in the valley, such as the rearing of the tawny owlets and jackdaws, and the occasional passage of foxes and roe deer along the stream.

Frances was not able to be with me as near the sett as this, because her Australian visit and the time taken up by her job had broken her contact with the badgers, and they were no longer familiar with her scent. She often watched from the ledges and would exchange comments with me as we walked home. There was the evening when people were working late in a field at the edge of the woods, the sounds of hammering and shouting coming noisily at times to our quiet valley. At these moments all the badgers except Jack would bolt into whichever hole was nearest and stay there for a few minutes. Jack would pause and look and listen and then go on snuffing into my wellingtons or pockets. Frances said afterwards, 'I expect he saw that you didn't mind the noises and said to himself, "It's all right if *she* doesn't run away!" '

He also developed an engaging, almost irresistible way of whickering at me for raisins, as a pony does for oats.

The beech tree hole was in frequent use by the cubs and their mother, as well as the yearlings, perhaps to give the main sett a rest and airing. The old boar was not in evidence at all at this time. Perhaps he, too, felt in need of rest and an airing. As far as I could learn from my observations there, the beech hole was certainly connected under-

71

ground with the upper and lower side holes, but not with the main sett itself.

I tried now to move around a bit so that I could get more interesting photographs; the badgers never knew where they were likely to find me and would come out and cock their ears and snuff the wind and wait for me to call quietly, 'Come on, badgers!' Piglet, as ever, was most co-operative, and one of my notes says, 'Piglet played up very well for me. I took about ten photographs of him foraging around a tree stump where I had hidden some currants.' Another note says, 'Piglet played delightfully with Ulysses, jumping right over him three times and once on to him. Jack, on my knee, tried to tug my nut-pocket away.'

That was the night, I remember, when I heard piteous screams in Valley field and a few minutes later a fox passed behind me carrying a hare. Such are the joys and sadnesses of those who would live close to the wild. I do not mean that I blame the fox; it is in fox nature to hunt for a living, and is much more in harmony with the natural order than nearly all the ways of man. I mean that it can be, for us, a hard lesson to learn this truth and to watch with a quiet heart and mind and if possible not interfere. But the cries of the victims never left me unmoved, however often I told myself that the only alternative for them would be an ultimate slow and wretched death by starvation, for all life is mortal.

'Ma, you are inconsistent,' Sean teased me. 'You tried to rescue Toddy and Arwen, and once you fed a whole litter of fox cubs when the vixen was shot, and you say try not to interfere!'

It is difficult to know what is best to do when the emergency presents itself. If Arwen had been left to die it might only have been nature's way of strengthening the badger stock by eliminating the weak. Perhaps I did the family no ultimate good in salvaging this small one who couldn't keep up with the others and couldn't stand the cold: but she was, by all appearances, a very fine sow when last I saw her. And those provisional words, 'if possible' – I don't think that it would have been possible for me to leave that cub to die, whether good for the family or not.

Perhaps another way of looking at it is that our race has tampered so much already with the lives and habitats of wild creatures, to their disadvantage: might it not be a proper thing for us to work a little towards their advantage when we can?

Reading my notes of the nights of June, so full of interest and delight, I am pulled up by my last entry: 'With much rain and wind and cold, June was the worst on record; no good weather this year since the last week of March.' And yet I had hardly noticed it! Protected by pullovers, wellingtons and duffle-coat and sitting on my rubber pad, I had been immune to the cold and wetness and receptive only to the enchantment of that valley.

I got some new, smaller wellingtons about that time but the badgers really hated them for some obscure reason, and would jump away in horror as their muzzles came in contact. I had no option but to go back to wearing my big old winter ones, meant for two pairs of ski-socks. These were checked with deep suspicion the next evening but finally passed as O.K., and with much relief on the part of badgers and myself equally. One does not care to give offence to one's friends.

The next day I was straining newly-made elderflower wine in which raisins had been soaking. These I carefully separated from the elderflowers and took along to the badgers in the evening. I was at the beech tree place and the family came at once cheerfully enough, sniffing my boots and finding them in order. I put down the winy raisins with some bits of bread and the badgers rushed to investigate. They were, to a badger, *horrified* by the smell – worse than new wellingtons – and kept rushing away. Only Roly, to my surprise (I should have expected it to be Jack) dared to stay long enough to pick out the scraps of bread. So it must sometimes be, that the harder we try

73

to please the more we find we have inadvertently offended!

When I was collecting our milk the next morning at Upper Highfield Farm, Vivien Abels, who lives there, told me that a badger was trotting down the Sandy Lane in front of her car a few nights before. She said to herself, 'I'll bet it's going to see Monica,' and, sure enough, it turned left and vanished up our drive!

'It knew your scent,' Bill said, when I told him. But, realist that I like to think I am, I couldn't help concluding that it was just a short cut off the lane in the direction of the valley.

Bill at this time was almost as busy as he usually had been at the farm. Now that the lawn area and his terrace and paths were finished he was beginning on an epic wall-building project, using our own beautiful Bargate stone. Many of the stones carried a mantle of moss which he was careful not to disturb, so that the walls had a built-in air of maturity. Our entrance from the old Sandy Lane had been cut deeply through an old hedge-bank and the walls curled in nine feet high, holding back the earth and diminishing as the driveway rose to the higher garden. A branch from the left-hand wall continued along the path at the back of the house to disappear into the ground at the highest level of the three-tier lawn to the south.

Meanwhile he was building himself a greenhouse and continuing with the kitchen garden and making nesting-boxes and sometimes finding time for his little wooden bowls.

As Jack grew out of true babyhood he became more and more inclined to throw his weight about. Often he would dispute the right to someone else's nut or raisin – even if that someone were the now majestic Proudfoot – snapping and turning very bossy and trying to get all for himself. Proudfoot, though now a big, sleek and shining boar, was not at all like that: even in what might be the equivalent of careless adolescence he had always been gentle and fair towards the others in the family. Jack still sometimes tried to tug my coat off – or me away. My notes say of one such evening: 'Managed to take several photographs, some at five feet, when cubs – i.e. Jack – calmed down.'

It was in this month of July that I did the stream photographs. Sitting on the opposite bank of the stream below the main sett I tossed my few peanuts – watched by wonderstruck badgers peeping over the rampart – and called to them, 'Come on, badgers! Come on, cubs!' Jack and Roly quickly responded and came down but would not pose for me. Jack's wet legs were a hazard to the camera as he galumphed on and off my knee and splashed into the water again, and away back up the valley-side to see if there were any scraps at our usual rendezvous. Eventually, and much more sedately, Piglet and Jess came down. Jess had always kept her distance, and had no intention of risking anything else, but Piglet, ever obliging, stepped into the water and drank slowly and neatly, so that I was able to wait for a prettily drifting leaf to come into the picture with him.

Sometimes I would get up at about four in the morning to be in the valley before sunrise. These dawn hours had a special magical quality, of soft quiet greyness merging into wet sparkle and birdsong and smelling like some unworldly elixir that Paris never knew; but the badgers were more nervous at this time of day and would not play riotously as in the summer evenings. Perhaps, after a night's foraging, they were a little tired and not as sharp-set for something to eat, as when they emerged from the day-long sleep. And I always grew very cold, however much I wore. The evening woods still held the warmth of the day, but dawn woods could be near to freezing, even in July.

On one such early morning I heard that unique unearthly noise that is a badger's yell. In all my years of association with badgers I have heard it only three times. Imagine a vixen's shriek, triple it and add that certain eeriness that seems to stop the breath, and you have some idea of it. Frances thinks that it has a human quality, as does a vixen's shriek, but where the vixen sounds like a woman in terror the badger's yell has a masculine harshness. No one yet seems to know why badgers do it. A love-cry, a battle-cry, a pain-cry, all have been suggested, but in my experience none will do. I have heard it in the dead of winter, well outside the breeding season, and in the late autumn I actually watched a badger as he made this lost-soul crying, and he was trotting calmly along the path between the tree stump hole and the main sett.

Perhaps in the middle of winter one might – and once I did – confuse a badger's and a vixen's screaming, but vixens do not scream in spring and summer, and I have never heard them in autumn.

During this summer Puff had been away for some weeks but returned at the beginning of August. Although badgers continue growing up to three years old at least, they are sexually mature at one and a half and have their first cubs at two years. Puff, then, was in her first mating season; I realised that probably she had been away on a badger's honeymoon, although she brought no boar home with her. She came and nuzzled my hand, just as in the old days, and I wondered if presently she would be gone again to join the gentleman of her choice.

There was an evening about this time when Roly was not with the other cubs, but on my way home at dusk she trotted out of the woods ahead of me on to my path. I stood still and dropped a few nuts, wondering how she would react to meeting me so far from her home ground, but she came up calmly and ate my offerings. I leaned down with nuts in my open palm and she took them from my hand; then when these were gone and I was upright she too raised herself and planted her front paws on my thigh, as a big cat would, and ate from my hand as I stood up straight.

Proudfoot was the next yearling to go away, but Shy and Ulysses were still nightly at our meeting place with Puff and the little ones. I seldom saw the parents now.

On daytime walks I used often to visit outlying setts in the hope of seeing signs of occupation, wondering about roving yearlings, and the cubs of earlier years, such as Arwen's family. One sett about half a mile downstream was clearly in use, with fresh digging to be seen and pathways scraped by recent passage of bedding bundles. I watched here once or twice and saw the two occupants, but neither was known to me. My guess was that the absent badgers, if they had escaped the perils of the London-Portsmouth road, were over at Upper Highfield Farm, which is part of the valley badgers' extended territory, but Frances and I did not watch there very often as the setts were close enough to the road for traffic noise to spoil the evening's pleasure.

The proximity of this road – then in process of becoming a dual carriageway – also painfully brought home to us the danger that it was to badgers crossing to and from setts in Forestry Commission woods at the other side. When these new roadworks were at the planning stage, those of us in the district who cared about the badgers' safety had asked for an underpass at their main crossing place, pointing out not only the hazard to badgers but the risk to human life. It is no fun for a motorist travelling fast and perhaps with his family in the car, to hit a thirty- or forty-pound badger. Indeed, a series of mysterious fatal accidents did occur along this stretch of dual carriageway from the time that it was first opened.

If we had foreseen the long struggle we were to have, involving more and more well-wishers, some from far outside our area, while the badgers continued to die on the road, we might have felt a little faint-hearted. Over the course of our three-year negotiations for the underpass seven badgers lost their lives at this place, and these were only the ones we knew about. How many crept away injured, to die in ditches and corners, no one will ever know.

CHAPTER 11

Proudfoot came back at the end of August, and seemed as pleased to see me as I was to see him. 'He came to me at once, placing his front feet on my knee, as always,' I wrote. 'Jack of course rushed across and tried to break it up. I had to be careful. Earlier he took my thumb and pulled my hand away from my knee, but it was a gentle hold and left no toothmarks.'

There are many comments on Jack's bumptiousness about this time. 'Jack shoved around, as he always does. Again I had to be careful.' 'Jack very pushful; when I stood up he tried to climb me. I felt like a honey-tree.' (We used to spread honey on the trunk of a particular oak tree and the badgers climbed up to lick it.) 'Jack very shoving as usual. Does not now mind being spoken to. Previously if he were too bumptious and I said firmly, "Stop it, Jack!" he would dash away, although not far. Now he doesn't dash.' 'Jack tried to rake my feet away when I was standing up!' The cubs, of course, often did this when I was sitting, in their indefatigable search for peanuts.

Jess, an elegant, beautiful little badger, remained very cautious. Shy, I noted, although as old as the mighty Proudfoot, 'is only about the size of this year's cubs and still very shy.' Now that surprises me, reading this two years later with Shy still at the main sett, the biggest badger there and no longer shy. I had forgotten what a slow starter she was.

Hula was bringing in such a bounty of rabbits that I began taking the odd one along to see if the badgers fancied it. They are reputed to dig up nests of young rabbits, but are not fast enough to catch rabbits in the field. The first one I put down beside me at a sitting place between the north and lower entrances and against the honey-tree; I was only a few feet from either entrance but had been accepted there with no reservations.

Jack, Piglet and Roly came out at once, followed by Jess and Shy and Ulysses. The cubs were horrified by the dead rabbit, averting their eyes in a most comical way ('Oh, Mummy! There's something horrid in the woods'), then looking again and jumping back from it; but Shy picked it up and took it into the lower hole. The cubs' mother appeared from somewhere in the woods behind the sett and circled around for a while but as usual would not come near. Had she 'received' the anxiety feelings of the cubs? I had not seen her previously for some days.

My surprise at the bold Jack's fear of the dead rabbit was quickly corrected when the next night I took the hindquarters of a Hula catch. After a few cautious sniffs he grabbed it firmly, as one grasps a nettle, and marched head-high into the sett with it while the others looked on in an admiring, even awestruck way. And so it continued with every surplus Hula rabbit I took with me.

In September I wrote, 'For the first time ever both Jess and Ulysses ate from my hands, though warily. Jess didn't know *what* to eat, whether fingers or scraps. Ulysses champs, so that I have to be careful. Of this lot only Puff and Proudfoot and Roly can be really relied on to be gentle eating from the hand. All the cubs followed me up to the track. Rover met me in the glade and came home with me.'

The badgers were putting on weight for the winter, as is natural for them to do, even Shy looking better than she had done all summer, less scruffy and her coat shinier and smoother.

The cubs were very disrespectful towards my wellingtons, scraping them from side to side to look under them, and Jack took to pushing his muzzle down inside, where once a peanut had fallen. I took some photographs of these doings but it was rather difficult as I had to lean back so far to get boots and cubs in focus, a thing that obviously amused a pair of field-glass watchers at the other side of the valley. One knew the problems of wild-life photographers trying to get near enough, but the problem of trying to get far enough away was one less likely to be encountered.

The year moved into October, with night after night of quiet woods and soft weather and tumbling badgers who honoured me with their absolute trust. An entry taken almost at random reads: '6.25 on track. Torch in the ash tree. I called and Jack and Piglet came from the valley, pausing to drink at the hollow in the birch. Roly and Jess came rollicking after them. Enchanting grooming scenes, all the cubs together; wished I'd had the camera but weather unsettled. Falling leaves swirling in torchlight. Roly came back with me as far as the glade, where Haile was waiting to escort me home.'

And another: 'Seven badgers by moonlight; all the cubs and three yearlings. Puff came on to my knee – she is very big for this! How dramatic moonlight is in the woods; the black trees slashed with white from crown to roots. There are few greys; everything is black or brightest silver.'

There were rainy nights when drops sparkled on the twigs and in the torchbeam, and I saw rain running off the badgers' coats as off a thatched roof; they are wonderfully waterproofed. In thick mist the torchbeam looked almost tangible, a cloth-of-silver curtain; Proudfoot once reached up to sniff at it. Sometimes on clear nights when moths flew in the beam he would take a swipe at them.

Now that we were well past the owlet season I was having trouble with Haile again. Sometimes when Frances was with me she would take him back home, to his fury, or to walk in a different direction. But when I was alone I could do little and heard with resignation his miaow of greeting as he stalked out of the woods to join me. These cubs could not have had much acquaintance with him in the months when he had waited for me in the glade and

Inner Wood, and they were at a loss now as he squared up, hissing like water thrown into a hot frying-pan. The first time, after staring at him for a minute in the torchlight they turned and ran back to the valley, all except Jack who stood up to the challenge until Haile stalked closer and hissed again, then Jack too retreated.

I went to great lengths to elude this fiercely defensive cat as so often I had done before, taking devious and different routes to the valley, but there were always the evenings when he was already there before me. Sometimes I would give up a night's watching and take him home at once, but there were times when I just hoped he would learn to tolerate these other animals and live with them at peace. I could not help remembering the day when he had so idyllically played with Arwen, the first of my friendly badgers.

Rover, of course, was a quite different proposition, as I have written earlier. He is a large cat in every aspect of the word; in his physical form – from whichever angle he is viewed, it makes little difference; in his sheer presence, weight and appetite and in his ways, which are largely tolerant and loving. He presented a lesson, ignored by Haile, in the art of animal relations. Although now in middle-age, Rover still had much energy and play left in him; his partial retirement from long walks gave place only to a more faithfully observed ritual of meeting us whenever we had been away from the house. In all weathers and temperatures he would be the first thing we saw on walking or driving up to our high garden. His shining black fur spangled with rain or frosted with snow, he would be there, stepping to meet us in the curious way that he had of moving both legs on one side in unison, like a camel or a pacing-horse; one always marvelled that with his bulk he did not fall over. He would pound the path in his pleasure at meeting us, his huge paws, from which tufts of hair sprouted, spreading like falcons' feet; his splendid tail, a black ostrich boa, waving high.

With all his gargantuan appetite (which for his sake we

do not much indulge) Rover has curious fancies. Above most things he dotes on plain boiled potato, and if the larder door is left open will climb shelves to reach this delicacy. Cold cabbage is delicious and beetroot nearly as desirable. Carrots and sprouts too are held in high esteem. Meat is good, but not rated much higher than the more favoured homegrown vegetables. For yeast tablets he will open the tin and put his paw in, raking them out, or with a swipe he will knock the tin over to scatter the tablets on the floor – a race then between him and the rest of us to stop him eating more than his share: all this to the mystification of Hula and Pardos who think even the smell of these things disgusting.

One who does understand this fancy is Haile, but nothing will induce him ever to open the tin for himself. There are some who say that he cannot open it, but we sneakingly think he considers this work below him. He sits beside Rover waiting for him to tip the tin over and then will swoop into the tablet race against us. He is the most outrageously arrogant cat we have ever encountered, and is known to my grand-daughter Lindsey as H.R.H.. Frances and I think that he looks on Rover the Woodpile Cat as his gentleman's gentleman, whose mission is to serve, wash and wait on H.R.H. In his large gentle way Rover does not mind playing the part. He is my daughter Shelley's favourite cat, and she approves of his figure. 'Outside every fat cat,' she says, misquoting Cyril Connolly, 'is an ever fatter cat trying to get in.'

In some ways Rover is more doglike than catlike – in fact is often called The Dog, although that is not the reason of his name (I told the story of the naming in an earlier book and shall not repeat it here). His faithful devotion, sometimes ecstatic affection, and unfailing meeting of his people, are doglike qualities, and I appreciate them. All the same, Sean and I have a special admiration for Haile's truly catlike proud independence, calling no man master.

Considering his size and clumsiness, Rover's choice of a bed is rather funny. Much his favourite place is the high wooden stool in the kitchen, now usually known as Rover's four-poster. Its hard oval seat is smaller than Rover curled up at his tightest, so that he looks like a kind of black flying saucer, or hovercraft, the furry whirl of progress overlapping the stool all round him.

It was a pity that it had not been Rover rather than Haile who elected to share my badger watching hours. With Rover I think there might have developed some quite splendid inter-species relations, cat, badger and human enjoying each other's company.

Whenever Frances had days off that autumn and winter we would, as in the year before, go down to work in the valley. We felt very much amateurs at woodland management but clearly some things needed doing, such as the removal of dead branches and coppice, the clearing of paths and maintenance of fences. We didn't want to 'garden' the wild valley, but where fallen trees had left gaps we thought it proper to plant young trees of kinds natural to Surrey woods.

This was one of the most fascinating and absorbing jobs I have ever done. We walked and climbed in the steep woods, always searching for shapely saplings growing in places where they had no chance of full development, such as on the edge of a path or too close to another tree. We looked for oak and beech, holly and ash and lime, all native to our valley, but especially we liked finding little beech trees; they had such grace and symmetry always, even when very young. In their prime we thought them magnificent, with the grace no other woodland tree possessed. They carried the crown, too, for sheer glory of colour; a green in spring so delicate and full of light that one marvelled to see it, and in autumn golds and coppers of rare splendour.

No one had worked much in the valley in our farming years, unless it were to cut out a bundle of bean-sticks. Old clumps of coppice hazel had died back for want of cutting, but still darkened the woods with their crowded drooping poles so that often we would walk through an area several times before suddenly one of us found in the shadows a little tree almost crying out for transplantation.

We had our planting days and our clearing days. Clearing was very hard work, tough on hands and shoulders; dead wood is often much harder to cut than green wood; but it was no good bringing in the young trees without letting in light for their growth by cutting out the dead and dying.

Anything bigger than pole-size we left alone however dead and crumbling; such trees make perfect homes for many kinds of wildlife, from woodpeckers and owls to woodlice, all of them a part of our world. After a tidy initial burst of building woodpiles with our trimmings we turned to the more natural way of breaking up everything small enough and leaving it on the ground to rot and eventually return in its proper cycle to woodsoil, the substance of more trees. Only the paths we kept clear, so that we could walk quietly at night, disturbing no wild creatures.

Friends who knew of our tree-planting sometimes gave us saplings which they had themselves rescued for us. Two little oaks, doing nicely now, were presented to me in Sussex by ten-year-old Martin Gasson, after he had heard about the work in the valley. It was entirely his own idea. Several wild cherries and two more oaks came from our old friends Pat and John at Cosford Mill. Natalka gave us a yew and a sycamore; the sycamore – rescued from a building site – we viewed with mixed feelings, as it has a reputation for taking over woodlands with its seedlings, but it was a beautiful little tree and we decided to give it a chance.

It was only at the end of our first season of planting that we realised our mistake in not taking into account the roe deer. In early spring, roe bucks begin to clear their newly grown horns of the protecting 'velvet' which grows on them, and they do this by rubbing them against small trees and brushes. This is called fraying, and when you have seen the effect on the little trees you know why. A sapling favoured as a fraying-stock has no future at all. Frances and I grieved as we walked the woods one spring morning to look at our plantings, and found many of them standing in ribbons of white stripped bark, like ravaged sylphs who have been left helpless in their torn dresses.

Clearly we must do something quickly if we were not to lose most of our saplings, for roe bucks will go on fraying throughout the summer, even when the velvet has gone from their horns; there is a second purpose, that of marking territory. Each sweep of the buck's head against a sapling smears scent from glands in the forehead, and as the summer moves towards the rutting season in July and August these glands become more and more active. We had lost young trees, but as with most of life's misfortunes we had at least learned something: the important thing was not the number of trees we planted but how well they were protected. Next winter instead of putting in six at one time we would plant two and surround them with posts and wire-netting, but meanwhile the survivors of this year's planting had to be safeguarded.

Over the matter of fencing we had many thoughtful moments. Naturally we did not want to shut people out of the valley; but wherever one goes there are vandals – in our case people with uncontrolled dogs, people who shoved branches down sett-openings, broke trees, lit fires and picked or trampled on rare flowers – and how can one exclude these and not the careful ones? I had seen the valley badger cubs fleeing in terror and danger from a large pursuing dog, and once was enough.

This, actually, was a strange story which I may as well relate, however improbable it sounds.

Some years ago, before I was on familiar terms with the badgers, I was watching on the ledges with Sim and Barnabas, nephews of an old friend and on half-term holiday from school. I had my camera and long lens on the tripod and had been taking photographs of the cubs playing around the rampart.

It was a perfect June evening, warm and soft and full of bird song; the cubs were exuberant, their mother peacefully watching them, as so were we. When finally they all began to trot through the darkening woods together it seemed as if nothing could be wrong with their world.

85

Then suddenly it all blew up in barking and rushing and yikkering as the sow and cubs raced back to the sett in a panic, a large retriever-style dog close at their tails.

We were horrified. It hadn't seemed possible that Eden could collapse in ruins so soon. I had begun leaping down the dug-out steps and across the stream without stopping to think. The badgers were now underground again, the dog raking at the sett entrance; it was too dark for me to be sure if any of the cubs had been hurt, or even if all were safely back. Pounding up the other side I was forced to stop for breath, and then saw in the dusk a most unlikely man – at least for those times of more conventional dress. Tall and thin he wore a kind of cowboy hat and a curious jacket. In one hand was a coil of rope and in the other a stick, or possibly a gun. The light was now so dim and I so outraged that I did not register all the details carefully. I rushed on and stood blazing up at him, telling him what I thought, and suddenly to my amazement realised that now I was blazing *down* at him. I hadn't seen, or anyway taken in, his change of position, but there was no doubt about it – he was lying down, just in front of me with his cheek in one supporting hand like a person on a beach. All he had said was, 'I thought they were anyone's woods.'

By now Barney had come charging up the valley-side to support and if necessary protect me. Sim, I found, had stayed to look after my camera equipment, both actions absolutely typical of both boys, I thought later. After a few minutes, my anger exhausting itself, I perceived that our man had risen and was moving off into the dusk, the dog with him. I turned to Barney. 'Can we have dreamt it? What were the rope and stick for? And *was* it a cowboy hat?'

'I thought the stick was a gun,' he said, 'and it could have been an old-fashioned scout hat.'

By now Sim had reached us with my equipment, and we spent an anxious hour searching the woods around with my small pocket torch, in case some injured cub might be lying there, but we found nothing. I decided to make a dawn visit to the sett and see if all the cubs were there.

On the way home we tried to make sense of the odd events. In the end Barney decided, 'I think he was a bit mad – the funny clothes. And a potential suicide, taking along a rope and a gun in order to have a last minute choice of methods. His lying down fits in, too.'

I was still puzzled. 'Do you think he could have lain down out of insolence, or do you think his legs just gave way because I was so angry?' We never did find out any of these things, but in the early morning thankfully I counted all the cubs, and all of them seemed sound.

And so remembering this, and other outbreaks of irresponsible behaviour, we borrowed our usual tools from Bill and got on with the fencing. Sean painted a notice-board for us with courteous wording and we fixed it at the south end of the valley. Within weeks it was riddled with shot holes and before the summer was over it was in fragments scattered on the ground.

We let the matter of the notice-board lapse; perhaps it was just too provocative. But then, disturbing a man with a spade and terrier (after foxes, he said) at one of the outlying holes, we continued patiently improving the fencing.

We were not trying to keep the valley for our own personal pleasure, but for the animals and plants whose ancient home it was. We held it only as stewards, in trust for them.

The fencing was hard exhausting work; carrying the posts, making the holes with the heavy iron folding-bar, driving in the uprights and straining the wire. Sometimes I took an easier line for an hour or so and roamed off with Haile and my camera, while Frances unravelled and joined the old coils of barbed wire we had salvaged from earlier fences. There were always strange and beautiful flowers to photograph; great broomrape and toothwort, orchids of different kinds, Solomon's seal and figwort, as well as the commoner but just as beautiful flowers. Then back to the fencing with energy renewed, and noting with excusable pride that our later stretches of work were much less awful than our first.

CHAPTER 12

During the autumn and early winter Puff and Proudfoot were away from the valley. Jess, too, no longer came to the meeting place, and I was never to see her again, nor either of the parents. But Proudfoot returned in early January; he was in fine condition and came to me just as he had always done. This was the quiet time of the year, as I had noticed in the two previous winters, when badgers are often late and lethargic or missing altogether. This January though was less blank than in the other winters because three of the yearlings were still at the main sett as well as the three cubs. The badgers were not really hungry now. Still fat from their autumn feasting and with the winter laziness on them, they picked and chose among my offerings with none of the old voracious scrapping over favoured bits, and often leaving before everything was eaten. They were also – as I have often found in winter – shyer and more reserved than usual. Even Proudfoot once or twice put down my stroking hand with his large paw as if simply not feeling sociable.

I tried to determine if Shy were pregnant but she seemed to be no size, really, although hungrier than any of the others. If she were going to have cubs they would probably be born in the following month.

Jack was the next absentee, and early in February I saw my best-loved of all the badgers, Proudfoot, for the last time. Haile and Rover were both with me; Haile excited, skirmishing around, and Rover sitting peacefully on the track blinking slowly to himself, the night, the badgers and me. Roly, Piglet and Ulysses were on the track, keeping well out of Haile's range, then Proudfoot arrived, calm and stately. Haile twice charged him, spitting furiously, but Proudfoot ignored him, continuing to eat the nuts I had scattered, neither giving ground nor troubling to retaliate. He came up to my hand and Haile again charged. I could not help but admire the courage of this cat, so much smaller and lighter than any badger and probably attempting to defend me as well as himself. Proudfoot may well have been a little annoyed, as a lion may be by a hyena, for he strode away and continued his foraging a few yards up the track. The other badgers had long since left, not liking Haile's dashes and hissings.

All this time Rover had remained completely calm with Proudfoot often very close; sometimes he washed a paw and sometimes he just went on blinking and looking at life and maybe, for all I know, thinking.

It is good that we are not aware of the future, even in comparatively small things, for I should have been sad if I had realised that this was the last I should see of Proudfoot.

Piglet was the next to leave. Now, of the ten badgers at the main sett in the summer, there were left only Shy, Ulysses and Roly.

Once I heard a quick chasing or scuffling noise in Valley field, with loud coughing grunts. This was the middle of February: were returning yearlings being driven off because of new arrivals? If so, who were the parents?

I was often enchanted, on these quieter nights, by a woodmouse whisking out of the shadows for crumbs and peanuts. On one night Rover, who was with me, rushed after it but happily failed to catch it.

There seemed little indication that Haile might cease or even slacken his hostilities towards the badgers, but for their part they began to grow indifferent to his threats, as Proudfoot had done before them. One evening early in March when the three regulars were foraging on the track, he stormed out of the woods and made several rushes at them, all ignored by them in what must have been a most maddening way. Provoked beyond endurance Haile rushed in again and to my anxious astonishment hit Ulysses in the face! Incredibly, this seasoned traveller just went on eating peanuts, and Haile came back to me, baffled and furious. A few minutes later, after ostentatiously stropping-up on a birch behind me, he suddenly pounced and caught a woodmouse which he carried all the way home, trotting beside me, and ate in comfort in the kitchen.

About this time I had one of those humbling experiences which, I like to think, happen to us all and no doubt are very good for us.

Frances was with me on the track, using her small pocket torch; we did not have the big torch hanging in the tree because there was a three-quarter moon. The badgers had gone up on the bank behind us and Frances turned on her elbow and shone the little torch up to them.

'Ulysses is in milk,' she said. 'I can see the udders.'

'Nonsense,' I said, 'Ulysses is a boar.' But I too rolled over and turned my little torch on this enigma. Frances was indeed right. 'Shy is in milk too,' I added, glossing things over.

'Never mind,' said Frances. 'I thought he was a boar, too. He – she – has such wide jowls and that scruffy thin tail. But anyway, how splendid! Two sows with cubs.'

'Have you thought,' I said on the way home, 'we can't call her Ulysses any more!'

For a time we deliberated on this re-naming problem. Something feminine that bore some relation to Ulysses. 'It'll have to be Calypso,' I said.

We tried this for a few days, but the more we spoke it the more it didn't seem to be a badger-worthy name. 'There's no one else, really, but Penelope,' Frances said, 'and that's not very badger-worthy, either.'

We settled for Penny, not liking it much, but Penny she became.

The situation in the main sett now was intriguing and different from any I had known before. There was no resident boar, nor even a visiting boar as far as I knew.

Two litter-sisters were in occupation, both with cubs, and the younger sister Roly was either with them or in another part of the same complex. Naturally there must have been a boar around at some time, but I had never seen him. Had he actually ever lived in the sett? If so, might he have died? Or been killed, perhaps on the Portsmouth road? Or been driven out because the sows got tired of him? Or had he never even lived in the valley – a light-of-love met fleetingly in summer woods over at Howlings, or down in the Punch Bowl, or anywhere else in these rolling woods and pastures? Was it even the same boar who had sired both these new litters of cubs? How little one knew, even after so many hours, months, years of watching, and how little it seemed one might ever know. I wondered where the older parents were: perhaps they too had been among the increasing casualties reported from the road.

Anyway, it was women's lib in our valley now, and re-membering the splendid fatherly boar of previous years I hoped the young mothers would manage all right with these their first cubs and not even a husband between them. Perhaps Roly would help, if she were allowed to do so.

It seemed strange, too, and perhaps regrettable to me, that out of the four two-year-olds the ones which had been friendliest – Puff and Proudfoot – had gone away, while the two who had been the more reserved had remained. I was glad to have Roly still in the valley. She alone of the three seemed really pleased to see me and to enjoy the friendly rub behind her ears and a stroking hand on her shoulder.

She too would presently be gone but I didn't know it, and meanwhile spring in the woods was delight enough. There was the earliest chiff-chaff I have ever heard – March 28th – and the woodcocks roding and glorious birdsong at sunset. The roe deer were active, running barking through the valley and in and out of the stream with bright splash-ing. Sometimes they came quite close to me without un-easiness and once all three lay down together very near to where I sat. One evening two of these three went racing

91

across the stream and up the further bank as if startled by something, their white targets showing. At the four-strand fence along the top they went over without visible pause and away into the chestnuts at top speed.

The third roe came from the woods behind me. She did not see me standing against the triple birch and came close, nibbling – alas! – wood anemones and sometimes elder. Penny was just emerging from the north hole of the main sett. She looked at the roe doe a few feet away and the doe looked at her but neither was greatly interested. The doe continued nibbling and Penny went back into the sett. Sows seem always more wary when they have young cubs underground. Shy, later, took slow and devious routes up to me, with several retreats.

Coming home I looked down from the higher fields and saw the mist lying thick like white smoke along the valley, and the cold was raw.

On April 9th I was greatly surprised and pleased by the return after many weeks of the bold bad badger, Jack. Even had it been possible not to recognise that champagne-bottle frontal stripe, there could have been no mistaking his bumptiousness and busy behaviour, but he was smaller than I should have expected. True to his character he left me when all the peanuts were gone. He was not as over-joyed to see me as I was to see him, and that was that.

The next evening my heart really ached for Jack and for Roly. I had still seen nothing of the new cubs and was waiting hopefully against the birch tree. In a few minutes Roly came up to me and I saw that she appeared to have been fighting – or worse, to have been attacked. Hair was missing from her left side stripe, there were scratches on her face and she looked generally scruffy – the lovely, elegant and sleek little Roly. Very soberly she took my offerings and accepted my caresses, then she went away southwards through the woods.

Next it was Jack, emerging from the beech hole and look-ing so subdued that I hardly knew him. He stood there uncertainly for a few minutes, suddenly saw Shy coming out of the north hole and with a quick scrabble turned and bolted back into the beech hole. Shy watched him vanish and then in a determined way walked up the path and went in after him.

Frozen with apprehension but able to do nothing I stood beside the birch tree, certain that somewhere down in the beech hole Shy was beating-up Jack. He was so much smaller still than even this small sow that I imagined him cowering in a corner in the darkness, unable to get away from whatever she might be doing to him. After a while she emerged and went back into the north hole, but although I stayed until after dark I saw no more of Jack; and not only on this night but never again.

These things were hard, but I did not blame Shy. The fact that her own, older parents had tolerated the presence of yearlings with the new cubs did not mean that these young sows would do the same. From everything one hears it is more usual for yearlings to leave and to stay away, whether of their own accord or because they are driven. This seems to me right and in the nature of things, since a territory will only support a given number of one species; if too many stay, all will suffer (why cannot the human species learn this truth?). Probably it was I who was to blame for the return and long stay of the previous yearlings, because of my small but regular offerings of tit-bits. Perhaps the young mothers were more anxious for their little ones, less easy going than the older generation. Besides, these were not their own grown-up children who were being ejected but their younger brothers and sisters.

One pleasing thing happened that night to lift my sadness. At dusk and under a half moon the two sows brought one cub up to me. It was the first of this litter that I had seen. They made low purring noises to it and the cub yikkered back. It was too dark to see which sow appeared to be the mother but she very soon dragged it back to the north hole and then inside, the cub yakking loudly. The second sow stayed around, not minding when I walked away out of the wood.

Three days after this I saw Roly once more. I was standing against the birch tree beginning to give up the idea of seeing the cubs that night: I had heard them the night before. Penny and Shy had been in and out collecting bits of bread and taking them down to the cubs but now the valley was silent again, as silent as woodland ever is; the innumerable small noises natural to such places have a quality of silence about them. Then through the twilight a badger came trotting fast down the path along the far side of the stream, through the gleaming water and straight up to me. It was Roly. I bent down and stroked her head and gave her all that I had left in my pockets. She was so confiding and friendly that I could not help but believe she was glad to see me. Certainly she must have realised how pleased I was to see her. I couldn't know when presently I watched her dumpy tail bobbing away down the valley that as so often with wild creatures I should not see her again.

There is sadness as well as joy in living close to wild animals: so much, so often is for the last time.

The two young sows seemed to be especially nervous for these first cubs. On the next few evenings they emerged with caution, making several attempts to come up to me but changing their minds and hurrying back, until eventually one or both would slip away quietly into the night woods with not another sign of any cubs.

It was already dark one evening when Penny came to me for nuts, and she was eating from my hand when I heard the sound of an approaching badger in the woods. Penny at once rushed to intercept and then came back alone. The visitor could not have been Shy, who was still underground. I wondered if it were Roly being driven away; or possibly Jack, or any of those four.

The next night, at half-past ten in clouded moonlight, both sows brought their cubs out of the sett and with much whickering up the path to me. There were at least three cubs altogether but the light was not good enough for a certain count. They were taken back after only a minute or so by Shy, Penny lingering for a few more scraps before trotting after them.

As seemed to have become usual this was another very cold spring. 'Continuous north-east system,' my diary says after weeks of chill weather. Except for one very brief emergence of two cubs, who were immediately pushed in again by Shy, I did not see any more of the family until the end of April, when four were brought up to me. Almost at once three were chivvied back, but one remained for a while with Shy. Would I ever know which young belonged to which mother in this strange ménage? Did even the cubs know, I wondered, who was who's mother?

CHAPTER 13

On the last day of April I had better luck. Arriving soon after eight I tossed some peanuts down towards the sett and called, 'Come on, badgers!' First came Penny from the copse behind me, her muzzle muddy and coat wet; it had been raining all day until mid-evening. Then Shy, from across the rampart, also wet and muddy. They took scraps of brown bread into the sett but peered suspiciously at a piece of white bread, a thing I seldom included. After sniffing at it and pushing it about a bit they ignored it until I picked it up and held it out. Penny took the piece with what I can only call a reproachful look and trotted a few yards to dump it in the bluebell leaves, as one who might say, 'You *know* we don't like it.'

At nine o'clock the cubs came out. It was too dark to count them but there seemed a lot, yikking and bouncing near the honeytree. There was much purr-whickering from the sows; it sounded rather like rattle-snakes. I hoped the whole family would be brought up to me but all were pushed in except one, which the sows brought to me. This one was very bold, reminding me of Jack. It was amusing when as it came closer I saw that it had a champagne-bottle stripe. I tossed a few raisins and it jumped inches and growled, but soon was within hand's reach (though I took no liberties) and enjoying the raisins. To this bold cub I granted provisionally a name and a gender. Probably male, I called him Jas, partly because he was so like the engaging wicked Jack and because this name—for James or Jasmine—could be switched if there were a mistake about the sex.

16. The old Sandy Lane

17. Frances fencing in the woods

18. Shy

19. Penny alias Ulysses

20. Piglet

21. Roly

22. Talley

23. The big, bad badger, Jack

Early in May the cubs grew more bouncy and were grudgingly allowed a little more liberty, but not every night! It was strange how sometimes perfectly natural woodland sounds would alert all the cubs into a bolt for the sett, such as on one evening when they were having a splendid knock-about on the rampart – one threw itself at the honey-tree and flopped back with legs waving – and just then a tawny owl flew overhead shrieking 'Quick! Quick!' as tawnies do. The cubs rushed back into the north hole growling and barking, and Shy who had been watching the games stood a moment and then followed. I think cubs may not have much inborn knowledge of what is safe and what is dangerous; they have to learn. Probably anything strange and noisy is dangerous at first (I have seen cubs dive at the clamour of a blackbird and the passing of the deer), and anything quiet and still (myself, for instance) is safe.

On this day I saw the first swallows, much later than usual. Cuckoos were rare as kestrels and, as for some years past, there were no nightingales.

May continued very cold with little cub activity until the tenth, when the strange business of 'farming out' the little ones began. It was dark except for shadowy moonlight when Penny brought one cub from the sett. Both rootled around me for some time until Penny stopped and stared towards the track. I could hear nothing and for a moment I was afraid that Roly or another of the yearlings might be approaching only to be furiously repelled again, when suddenly Shy appeared with the remaining three cubs. There were general greetings, as if these four had been away for days, with great tumblings of cubs in the shadows, and then followed for me an enchanting hour.

All six stayed close around, the cubs nosing, licking and chewing my boots and coat and climbing over my legs. As I sat on the woodland floor among them all, one 'walked the tightrope' along my outstretched leg, starting at the ankle and wobbling up past my knee. The sows fussed around like mothers at a toddlers' party, whickering and

97

nuzzling, and the cubs were very obstreperous. My notes finish, 'Very cold but thrilled, I crept away at about half-past ten.' But I remember I was asking myself questions. Where had Shy and the three cubs been? Were those three her cubs, and the fourth one Penny's? Had I really seen, in the dim light, a wound underneath Shy's throat? If so, had she received it in more fighting with the yearlings? What, if anything, should I do about it?

The next evening, hoping for some answers, I was near the birch tree just after eight. Penny was already there waiting and she watched me settle down. Shy came out of the sett a little later but I did not see her closely. First she and then Penny went trotting purposefully down the track towards the glade. It was a true case of Back in Ten Minutes, for that was the time they took before returning, with two cubs only which must have spent the day – their 'night' – somewhere from the glade sett to Inner Wood where there were several single holes and one large one known as the holly sett, all in the possession of this valley family and not regularly used. One of these two cubs was Jas, the other had a broad frontal stripe and I thought might also be a male. They both came to me readily, as the night before, and enjoyed a few currants before the sows took them into the sett. My hope for their return with the other cubs was not granted; I went home puzzled, and also a little troubled for I had seen that there was indeed an injury under Shy's throat.

The next evening all was normal, with the whole family at the main sett, and so it was the night after. But on the third night only Shy and one cub were there. I gave Shy a Hula rabbit which she took underground with the cub. The wound under her throat was spreading and looked infected, I thought, and decided to ask my vet about it.

Presently, seeing there was nothing more doing, I left, and as I walked through Inner Wood noticed through the trees a badger going along the edge of the wood and into the holly sett. Thinking it might be Roly I waited, but presently the badger emerged and I saw that it was Penny with one cub, which must have been inside the holly sett. They went back together towards the main sett, and so did I, though along a lower path and more slowly than the trotting badgers. When I arrived back at the sett Penny and Shy and two cubs were disappearing up the stream path. Where were the other two cubs? Baffled, I went home, pondering on this mystery of the disappearing cubs. I had seen nothing like it before.

I talked to my vet the next day about the worrying sore under Shy's throat, trying to describe it accurately. He thought that the trouble was its inaccessibility to her licking tongue, and that probably because of this she was scratching it, and he gave me some antibiotic powder to give to her in food.

I did think about the rightness or otherwise of giving medicine to a wild animal, and whether really I ought to leave it to nature. I decided to wait a few days and keep an eye on the sore, but I knew that if it continued to fester I should not be able to stand by and do nothing.

For a week the affair of the vanishing cubs abated and all remained at the main sett. I was glad because I wanted to try for a much closer contact with Shy, and this would involve the whole family. Now that it seemed likely that I should have to persuade her to take a course of medicated tit-bits, and probably even be forced to try to treat the wound externally, I needed to be on much more familiar terms with her. She had always been the shyest of the badgers – though less so now – and was the last one I would have chosen for such a job as this.

'Why did it have to be Shy?' I said to Bill. 'Any of the others I could have coped with – Puff, Proudfoot, Penny, Roly, Jack, even Piglet.'

At least I was glad that it was the owlet season, so that Haile would be unlikely to come far enough to complicate things more.

My plan was to go with the badgers where they went, if they would allow it and for as long as I could keep up, instead of just staying around the sett and watching them go. My first venture in this direction met with unexpected success for a first attempt. The cubs had been friendly, climbing about over my legs and jacket as I sat near the sett – and I was very near now, leaning against the honey-tree – just as if I had been a member of the family, while the mothers brought in a bundle or two of fresh bedding or just sat gazing peacefully down the valley.

When finally the family moved off as usual, towards Valley field, I rose and began to stroll leisurely after them. They had been accustomed to seeing me get up and walk away in another direction but not to my actually following them. The sows turned round and looked at me for a minute, and I stopped too and bent to scratch the wood-soil as a badger does; to alter a well-known phrase, when living with animals, do as they do. This seemed all right to them and they moved on, rootling here and snuffing there. Keeping my yard or two of distance I moved on too. We reached Valley field with no panic, on the contrary with much interest from the cubs in my own amateur foragings, so that now and again I allowed myself to 'uncover' a few raisins for them. The sows began to set a good pace through the tussocks and broomy thickets of this steep field as if purposefully making for a planned foraging ground – probably the oak woods to the south – and I did my best to keep up without making a disturbing noise or any appearance of being in pursuit. All went well until the field fence stopped me; I could get through it only by lying down and carefully rolling, complete with camera and equipment, but the badgers just ducked and ran under. By the time I was through and on my feet again I had no idea where they were in the twilit bracken waving in the wind. No matter, I thought to myself happily, enough for one night, and I went home over the wooded hilltop and the swooping fields.

After a few evenings I became more adept at foraging with the badgers – to the wonderment one evening of three people with field-glasses across the valley, to whom probably I seemed an eccentric modern Mowgli – and on

two nights managed to negotiate really rough valley journey-
ings involving climbing over, under and around the fallen
trees that block these steep woodland paths in so many
places; but of course inevitably I got left behind and stood
entangled listening to the exuberant rushing departure of
these badgers to whom the wild woods were as our gardens
are to us.

By the end of the week I was, as far as I could see, a
reasonably proper badger and it was as well, for two things
called for my badgerness. Shy's wound, after a day or two
of looking better, was festering so badly that there was no
longer any question about the need for treatment, and the
vanishing of the cubs had begun again. I was pitched into
both problems together.

The powder my vet had given me would not harm the
cubs through the mother's milk, he had told me, nor even
if a cub were to snatch and eat some; but it both looked
and smelt unpalatable, and although Shy would now at
last eat quite calmly from my hands without her usual
jumpiness I had not yet tried her with anything of an un-
natural flavour or in a dish. I made her a brown bread
and honey sandwich – like most badgers she loved honey
and Bill often gave me scrapings from his hives – and inside the plentiful honey I concealed the prescribed one
teaspoonful of powder. I then cut the sandwich into small
cubes and put these into a cat-dish, on account of the
stickinesss.

At the sight of the dish in my hands Shy was at once
suspicious and began her old nervous jumpiness. I tossed
her a sandwich cube when no cub was near enough to
grab it and cautiously she ate it. My problem now was to
interest her enough in the sandwich cubes without Penny
and the three cubs with her managing to snatch any. Several
times I had to shove the dish, in its plastic bag, down the
front of my jacket (looking no doubt like the fabulous
one-breasted woman) until free enough of roystering cubs
to try again. It was a case of tossing a few currants (they
last longer than raisins) in one direction for Penny and

the cubs, then quickly a honey-cube for Shy, until eventually she was close enough and brave enough to grab them from the cat-dish.

When finally Shy had eaten all her medicine for the night, and I had with feelings of triumph pushed the dish back into my jacket, I began to take note of the fact that I had not seen the fourth cub at all that evening. It was one which looked so like my loved Roly – and a little sow, I thought – that I had called her Robin, the names having first letters in common. I decided, instead of following the family, to go in search of this one lost sheep. The sows and three cubs looked back at me as they moved off into Valley field, seeing that I had not joined them, but after a minute they padded away and I trudged in the other direction, towards Inner Wood and the spare setts where the farming-out of the cubs had happened before.

Walking quietly by the holly sett, suddenly I saw a small white-striped face in the entrance. It vanished at once but I crept nearer and sat down and waited. Quite soon it was there again, snuffing the wind. I said, 'Robin! Come along, cub!' and she came hurtling down the rampart and straight to my hands as though saying, 'Oh, I'm so glad to see you! I thought no one was ever coming, and here I've been all by myself all day long!'

We sat together for a while and I gave her as many raisins as I thought good for her, and tickled her neck and let her clamber over me, and I talked to her a little and told her how beautiful she was: all very foolish of me, perhaps, but never mind. Then in the near-dusk I heard paws padding, and there was Shy coming down along the edge of the wood. I was so pleased that I gave her some extra tit-bits, and then watched her lead the cub away and back, I hoped, to join the others.

It seemed a hard upbringing, reminiscent of some old-fashioned English nurseries, this toughening of the little ones by leaving them alone – if indeed that was the reason. We all know how easy, even irresistible, it often is to suggest human motives for the actions of other species. But

102

badgers have to grow up in a hard world where many are against them; they must know every inch of their territories from the earliest possible age, lest some disaster should overtake the adults; they must be able to survive periods of hunger and know when quite young how and where to find their own food; above all they must be self sufficient and able to behave sensibly, by themselves, in dangerous situations. Probably again I ought not to have interfered, but a tiny snack and a few friendly exchanges could not seriously, I imagined, have undermined the sow's intentions, whatever they were.

The next night Jas was missing from the main sett, and also the one with a candle-flame stripe a little like Piglet. I managed to get all the medicated honey-cubes to Shy without as much difficulty as the first time, partly because of Jas's absence; he was so much the most rumbustious and greedy of the cubs; and as I sat with the family I began to think about names for the rest of the cubs. They had of course to be short names and easy to say, and to be equally applicable to males and females, remembering how fallible one can be in these matters. I had then much in my mind the great French statesman Talleyrand as I had been reading about him in view of going with my friend Aileen to the Loire Valley later that summer. It was, one might say, my Talleyrand summer, and so it was easy to think of dividing his name between the two anonymous cubs. I hoped he wouldn't mind. And so the candle-flame cub became Talley and the last one, whose stripe was widest just between the eyes, was Randy. (It was weeks afterwards and too late to do anything about it that my family told me Randy didn't just mean boisterous, as I had thought, but something much more sexy. I couldn't say this bothered me!)

Again I let the badgers go off foraging without me and again I went searching for my figurative lost sheep. There was to my surprise no one at all at the holly sett; at least, I couldn't believe that Jas, of all cubs, would not come out when I called him. So I went back on my tracks,

103

stopping to investigate and call at each of the single holes along the edge of Inner Wood. At the fourth two faces appeared in the hole, Jas and Talley, and there were the same ecstatic scenes that I had experienced with Robin, the cubs bouncing about me absolutely delighted to see someone that they knew.

After these events I never quite knew who would be at the main sett when I got there, or where – if at all – I should find the missing members. One thing is certain, these cubs must have learned their territory very thoroughly by the time their baby days were over.

There was one evening which caused me some anxiety because this time not only were three cubs missing but Shy herself, only Penny and Talley being at the main sett to greet me. My anxiety was because Shy's treatment had to be continued for three weeks without a break, any pause giving scope for resistant bacteria to develop. I felt I must find her at all costs for the evening's dosing. She was responding so well to the antibiotic, her wound drying up beautifully, that I was unwilling to let her miss a day.

I found her at the holly sett, the last on my tour of vacant holes, and all the three missing cubs were with her. I began to think that these three were all Shy's cubs, and Talley the only one belonging to Penny. We had a delightful starlit picnic under the beech trees, and if no one was really ecstatic at seeing me – since Shy was with the cubs – we all enjoyed ourselves for an hour or so until with whickering noises Shy padded away and the family rustled after her into the darkness.

CHAPTER 14

The affair of the vanishing cubs went on well into June. Sometimes I managed to find the absent young and sometimes I didn't; the territory of this valley clan is fairly extensive for regular patrolling, about two miles in diameter and with many secondary setts. On evenings when all the cubs were absent I noticed that the sows' udders looked full, as they would if there had been no suckling in the day, and I realised that this removing of the cubs was probably another way of weaning, as when last year's cubs had been left in charge of the yearlings.

Shy's festering wound was improving greatly after a week or two of treatment, and I had not seen any need of external dressing. She had taken a great fancy to her honey sandwiches and would now come actually running from the sett as I arrived and produced the little cat-dish. When cubs were present I had to take a great deal of care to make sure that they didn't snatch any of the sandwich, not because of any real risk to them but because the dose was necessary to Shy.

Haile mercifully kept out of the way, restricting his activities to the northern end of the woods. I had often feared to find him at the holly sett, which is in that area, but the gods were with me. Sometimes I would meet him on the way home and he would civilly join me. Once, quite near the holly sett, I encountered him hurrying through the woods carrying the haunches of a young rabbit. Exhibiting delight at seeing me and uttering muffled greetings through the rabbit fur, he fell in beside me and we went on together. He would have carried his catch all the way home, as he had done with the woodmouse, but it was heavy and after a while he allowed me to carry it for him. And in the end he didn't want it – presumably having eaten the main part in the woods. Rover enjoyed it enormously; he had largely given up hunting for himself since his woodpile days.

The sows' industry and enthusiasm in abandoning their cubs at lonely places began to increase, until sometimes I was finding each cub in a different sett while the mothers had the main sett to themselves. These youngsters were certainly learning independence. It was a relief to me when eventually as they grew bigger the cubs began to find their own way back to the home sett, and the sows, seeing that the game was up, abandoned it. Shy's dosing was over and her sore place healed, and I looked forward to a time of peaceful enjoyment in the valley. Very soon, however, Penny tried a new angle of parental heavy-handedness. If you can't stop a cub from coming home, she appeared to have reasoned, at least you can stop it from coming out; and for a time she engaged in this annoying tactic with Talley, the one I felt more and more sure was hers and her only one. Shy and the other three cubs would have been out for five minutes or more while Penny still sat at the north hole preventing Talley from emerging. One could almost imagine her saying to herself like some superior human mother, 'I'm not going to let my child play with *that* lot, as long as I can avoid it.'

Talley seemed a normal, well-built, healthy cub who bounced happily with the others when he was allowed. I tried to save a few scraps for him while this tiresome situation lasted, so that he wasn't deprived of treats as well as fun.

On June 8th a fox cub came through the woods and near to where I was sitting. It stood for a minute watching the little badgers playing and then slowly approached them, sometimes sitting for a moment or lying with its muzzle stretched along the ground towards them. I wondered as I watched if I was at last to have the pleasure

106

of seeing fox and badger cubs playing together. The little fox followed the romping badgers down the slope and right on to the sett rampart, but seemed uncertain about joining in. Eventually Penny made a slight rush at it and it went off through the trees.

The cubs were growing very confident and taking all sorts of liberties, such as rushing off with my gloves or rubber pad and jumping at my knees as I walked, like a lot of puppies. The gentle Robin, so reminiscent of Roly, had developed an amusing and uncharacteristic way of pretending to be very fierce when pouncing on a bit of food or another cub, swishing her little tail quite aggressively before the ultimate pounce.

Jas was often comical in his private games, as when one evening he dug up a small male-fern complete with root and rushed off into the beech hole carrying it like a toy. Or when he would jump into the air suddenly from all four feet and land on the same spot, but sometimes with the variation of spinning round in mid-air to land facing the other way. There was no doubt about Jas being the rough one of this family, just as his double, Jack, had been before. I had often to shove him away in order to protect my camera or my pockets or even keep my wellingtons on my feet; but I was fond of the rogue, as I had been of Jack. It is funny how engaging wickedness can be.

In the middle of June I had a visit from the broadcaster, Martin Muncaster, whom I had recently met at a World Wildlife Fund meeting. His suggestion was that we might make a tape recording in the valley for the BBC programme *The Living World*. We had talked about this over the telephone earlier in the day and I had suggested that he came along with Frances and me that evening just to see what went on, and then decide whether he would like to try a recording. I was not very enthusiastic. My own view was that there was not enough of audible interest, these woodland events being more of a visual kind, but filming had once been tried and abandoned because of the

107

difficulty of getting a generator into the valley. Also I was anxious not to have the badgers disturbed in any way, but Martin assured me that this would not happen.

When he turned up that evening I was dismayed to see that he had all his recording gear with him; I was sure that we needed a preliminary survey first and did not care for the thought of frightened badgers dashing away as we messed about with our unrehearsed arrangements. I didn't know Martin then, of course. He said patiently that something really interesting usually happened if he did not have his equipment with him, and that he wouldn't frighten the badgers. I knew well how the best things always happened when I didn't have my camera, so I said all right, we would have a try.

Martin is over six feet tall and must have found some of the places rather cramped that Frances and I slip through easily. However, we all got down to the valley, listening to his plan as we went. I had explained that the badgers did not make a lot of noise, and that although sometimes I spoke to them I naturally didn't say much. I couldn't see what there was for people to listen to. Martin said he wanted to try a kind of woodland interview between the two of us. He knew that the badgers wouldn't tolerate a stranger, so he had enough flex for a two-way system from across the stream, where he and Frances would be with the recorder. He would ask me about the badgers as they came to me, and I would hear (though the badgers wouldn't) through my headphones, and answer by a linked microphone. He thought that, as the badgers accepted so much, they would not greatly mind a few yards of flex lying across their ground.

I think I may not have been very co-operative at this stage but I fell in with Martin's plan. At the glade he and Frances turned off to cross the stream and approach from the far side while I went on as usual to the main sett, carrying my headphones. By this time we were late. The cubs were already out when I got there, which was a pity, as inevitably they detected the strangers coming along the

108

further stream bank and hurriedly tumbled back into the sett. But they had seen me, too, and were eager to discover what I had brought for them. It was a good thing for our plan that I had for some time been sitting so much closer to the north entrance, because now I had to stand actually on the rampart, as it was the only good foothold, endeavouring to catch the flex thrown up to me by Martin at the stream. This naturally involved some traffic-policeman armwork, to say nothing of splashing from below and other unavoidable noises. I caught the flex and, turning round, was astonished to see a yard or so behind me four little striped faces peering in wonderment over a root just at the sett entrance ('What *can* she be doing?') I walked past slowly with a reassuring word, trailing my flex, and the cubs bobbed back behind the root.

I had not long been settled with the headphones in place when the cubs trooped out again. Martin had been recording the sound of the stream, as opening music, and we had exchanged a few words to check the apparatus. The idea was that we were to go on for as long as the tape lasted – half an hour – if the badgers obliged, and the result could be edited down as required. The cubs and both parents played up splendidly, taking all in their stride with scarcely a blink, even the odd sight of their tame human hung round with headphones and microphone, and the way she kept on and on talking.

Shy came hurrying up as usual hoping for honey sandwiches and tripped over the flex, Jas bounced me and knocked the microphone sideways making a terrible noise that I had to explain, and all the cubs champed raisins close to it sounding like horses eating apples and then romped yikkering on and around my person. Between all this and whenever I could give my mind to it I answered Martin's questions and talked to the cubs and tried to prevent them from actually eating the equipment.

The tape ran out at about the same time as the peanuts and raisins so we trudged back, meeting at the glade to go on all together. Martin seemed pleased with what we had got, especially as I had been so pessimistic about how the badgers would react.

'It's as I once told her,' Frances said. 'They don't mind much what happens as long as *she* doesn't look afraid!'

We sat at the big kitchen table (brought with us from the farmhouse) and listened to a playback while drinking coffee and eating cherries and biscuits. There was plenty there to choose from, we agreed. The stream sounded beautiful, tinkling the programme in and out like a signature tune of the valley.

The Living World used all of it, and then repeated the broadcast on the following Christmas Day. I had such letters of appreciation, often from people oppressed by town living, that I felt overwhelmed and perhaps unworthy. 'It was a bright candle in a dark world,' one letter to Martin said. 'I have never enjoyed any listening so much. Thank you for this triumph.'

I knew I was lucky in having Martin for an interviewer; I have heard many and some are bullying and some cynical and some intrusive. He was none of these things and all of their opposites.

The day after the recording, the fox cub really did play with the badger cubs, so that at last I had seen this magical sight, but it was only for a few minutes, before Penny drove it away. The little fox returned three evenings later and made playful moves towards the badger cubs, but could not bring himself to take any more risks and trotted off towards Valley field.

CHAPTER 15

A long absence now interrupted my badger evenings, the longest since my watchings began so many years ago. First there was the Loire Valley journey and then, immediately I came home, an attack of flu that threatened to become pneumonia and would not clear up, dragging on to the end of September. Bad weather then prevented me from going to the valley for a few more days, until finally I wrapped myself up and tottered down there feeling unfit and a stranger.

That I was indeed a stranger I was soon to learn. I sat in my old place at the side of the track by the hazel clump and waited. It was early October and my torch was in the ash tree. A roe doe browsed along the track and a flock of wild geese flew over the valley honking in the starlight; they were heading, surprisingly I thought, north-eastwards.

A solitary badger came up the path by the triple birch and I saw that it was Penny. A few peanuts enticed her to move cautiously on to the track but she looked at me in a remote way and would not come to my hand. 'So soon does wildness return,' my notes say sadly.

The next evening was much the same, with one solitary wary badger, but this time it was Shy: and the third evening was like the others, but my visitor was Robin, who allowed me the honour of eating from my hand. Now I had resumed contact, however tentatively, with three of the badgers. They were the only badgers I was to see for all of that autumn and winter. What could have happened to Talley and Randy and that splendid ruffian Jas?

As so often, I felt frustrated at the little I knew and could know. Had they just gone wandering? Or – always the underlying fear – paid their tribute to the moloch dual carriageway? I should never know, but I looked carefully at the next victim brought to me from the roadside, afraid that I might recognise a champagne bottle-shaped frontal stripe, or a candle flame or a broad one between the eyes; but this one was a stranger, a young sow, perhaps from near Cosford Mill.

Through October Penny and Shy and Robin grew used to me again and forgave me for my long absence, but always I was looking for those other three who had gone away when I was not there.

The end of the month brought a crisis to our family that for a time eclipsed all other preoccupations, although it did not keep me for long away from the valley. As seems to happen to so many in these times, our daughter's marriage broke up and she came to us with her children Lindsey and Maurice. The new house seemed suddenly so full and lively that it was almost like the old farmhouse days. With five of us now always resident and Frances sometimes and Sean and his wife Saloshana whenever they could get away from their jobs, and occasionally old friends who didn't mind sleeping on the sofa or a camp bed or even the floor, we were often pretty crowded and it was surprising how happily everyone fitted in together. The animal population too exploded, as the children quickly acquired a zoo of mice, gerbils, guinea pigs, fish, stick-insects and rabbits, some indoors and some out, and naturally the zoo quickly expanded by its own amazing reproductive abilities. Our problem was one of Cats versus the Visiting Team, and now and again I am sorry to say the cats scored a goal. Shelley said it was evolution in reverse, for it was always the survival of the dimmest; the most intelligent (at escaping, anyway) being the ones that got eaten.

Rover, always so splendid at meeting and welcoming his people, now extended this loving service to Shelley, whom he came to regard with a special devotion. He had in full measure the mysterious ability, not uncommon in domestic animals, of knowing the times of arrival of his particular people. He could often be observed pacing past the windows with his strange camel-gait on his way to the front porch where, the rest of the family could be fairly certain, either Shelley or I would shortly appear and be greeted with genuine delight, to a waving of his plumy tail and a pounding of the doormat.

Bill with his practical approach to life's problems had seen a solution at least to pressures of human crowding and proposed turning the built-in double garage into two extra bedrooms. This might have seemed to be a daunting job, especially bearing in mind that he meant to do it himself, with only whatever help his ineffectual family might sometimes offer. Bill had never been daunted by seemingly impossible jobs and he drew up his plans. All of us helped at this, which was fun, but often we were more in the way when the real work began. We used to take our friends down the hall to see how things were getting on; the laying of the floor, the installing of the partition and floor boards and ceiling, the new window, the built-in wardrobes; all materialised as the winter went on.

Our friends were properly impressed by these works, and one, Mariota, even proposed herself as honorary painter and turned up regularly for this invaluable con- tribution. I remember with amusement how once when I was being interviewed for the BBC about the badger culvert, we all met in the hall; Mariota in paint-splashed jeans and old jersey, contriving to look frankly scruffy and beautiful at the same time, responded to my introduction with her quite naturally distinguished gesture and accent, 'How do you do? I'm the casual labour.'

The matter of the badger culvert had been gathering momentum during these weeks. The seventh victim had been brought to me from the A3, a yearling sow in beauti- fully sleek condition, probably from the Witley side of the road and a stranger to me. She had been picked up by Malcolm, son-in-law of my friend Pat Loarridge of Cosford

Mill. Pat and I decided that she should be photographed where she had died and we would raise public outcry if we could with the photograph.

First it was sent, with a letter, to a weekly paper covering this area. When it appeared I could hardly believe that it was the same photograph. I had photographed the badger lying on her back and showing a deep chest injury. This one was, incredibly, lying on her front and was so much over-inked and actually altered that one could not even see positively that it was a badger.

I telephoned the editor and taxed him with it. He was sorry, he said, if I was annoyed, but the print had been touched-up in their art department as it was felt that, left as it was, it might have upset the feelings of their readers.

I *was* annoyed. I had wanted to touch the feelings of the readers and I requested the paper to print a letter from me the following week, which in courtesy they did. The letter said: 'Sir, in defence of such reputation as I may have as a photographer, might I please be allowed to point out that my own perfectly sharp photograph of the badger traffic victim was considerably modified by your re-touching department in order, as you so kindly explained to me, to avoid harrowing the feelings of your readers?'

As our campaign for the underpass began to arouse interest more interviews were requested, including one on BBC television *Nationwide*, again with Martin Muncaster and held at the side of the dual carriageway. My photograph of the badger victim was shown on the screen at the end of the interview, bright, clear and faithfully sharp in every detail. I could only hope that the more sensitive readers of our weekly paper were not watching, or they surely were being harrowed.

Later another weekly, *The Surrey Advertiser*, very broadmindedly gave the photograph a large untouched showing, with under it another of Arwen eating from my hands and an article entitled, 'Seven Badgers Have Died'.

We had formed a small committee of involved people to decide on a policy, and it was agreed that we should

114

write a letter asking the Regional Controller of the Department of the Environment to receive a deputation with a formal request to approve the construction of one, or possibly two, badger underpasses at the main crossing places on this dangerous two-mile stretch of road. This was in effect the same request that we had made at the planning stages, when the cost would have been a fraction of what it would be now that the road was nearly completed.

The D.O.E. replied agreeing to receive us on a date in the middle of February, and meanwhile we planned and launched an appeal for public backing. Edward Bartlett, a Surrey naturalist and member of our committee, painted for us an arresting poster of a badger drinking at a woodland stream, and arranged to have a quantity of copies printed for distribution to shops and offices. We designed among ourselves a handbill with a space for signatures and distributed them widely with the posters.

Our campaign caught the imagination of people in this part of Surrey and over the border into Hampshire. People who had taken bundles of handbills brought them back signed and asked for more. We ran out of posters and had to get more printed. I talked about our project on BBC *Woman's Hour* and other programmes and answered many inquiries. When the day for our reception arrived we took with us more than two thousand signatures and the now well-known photograph of the seventh badger to be killed on the road; also detailed plans for a two-foot diameter culvert under the road and badger-proof fencing to run for 200 yards at each side of the culvert entrances.

We were graciously received and courteously heard as we stated our case. We made a particular point of human safety, because people who may not be deeply involved in wildlife at risk are concerned about human danger, and this was a very real danger. We said we realised that the cost of the work would be high at this stage, but reminded the Department that we had pressed for a culvert from the time of the original Public Inquiry.

I think we saw fairly soon that we had made a favourable

impression. We had after all reason and justice on our side. One cannot drive belts of concrete through wild places without thought for the creatures whose ancient homes these places are: one must not put night motorists in peril for their lives.

Three weeks after this meeting we received the news by telephone from the Regional Controller of D.O.E. The Department had agreed to put two culverts under the road, with supporting fencing at the sides; the work would be done fairly quickly as it would be undertaken by contractors who were working on the road at that moment.

We were, of course, absolutely delighted. 'Badgers Win the Day', said a newspaper headline. 'Plan to Save the Badgers', said another, reporting the meeting and its outcome. Perhaps the seventh badger had not died in vain.

This may all have seemed very splendid, and in many ways it was, but our culvert project must have been born when the stars were against it, so long did it take to get started and so many delays were there in its progress. As the months passed we made inquiries of the Regional Office at intervals, and always were told that work ought to be starting shortly but there had been difficulties with subcontractors and delays in the delivery of materials. New cubs had been born in the valley, and my hopes that they at least would have safe crossings of the A3 began to diminish.

A further bitter disappointment came in early summer, a time when inflation was really beginning to gallop. The D.O.E. looked at their constantly revised and increased costing for the two culverts and decided not, after all, to put in the second one until evidence was available that the first was being used by the badgers. Considering the long-drawn delays of culvert number one, this was particularly disappointing. How could one provide a report on unfinished work? And when would the work be finished? No one seemed to know; and as the delays persisted an eighth badger was killed on the road.

116

The second culvert had been planned for a very vulnerable crossing-place connecting a large active sett in the Forestry Commission woods with our own valley colony. Badgers had established an ancient track here between the two territories; it was the place where the television film had been made and where several badgers had been killed. Writing now, a year after our successful meeting in Guildford, the first culvert is at last finished; one scarcely dares to wonder whether, when the time comes, inflation will allow the second.

CHAPTER 16

All this time I had of course been continuing my watches in the valley, but as in previous mid-winters the badgers were quiet and unpunctual. Those present at the main sett were still only Penny, Shy and Robin, with no resident boar: but at the end of January Robin, alas, began to show marks of active persecution, so that I feared the older sows were trying to drive her away as they had the other yearlings, before the imminent birth of new cubs. The first thing I noticed was a bitten right ear, after which Robin was not at the meeting place for eight days. Then on the ninth day she returned but looking even more roughly treated, with bite marks on the side of her face and on her right flank, but she was self-possessed and ate calmly as usual from my hand. This was the last certain sign I saw of any attempt on the part of Penny and Shy to drive Robin away. I hoped they had now decided that she might be useful, after all. Both were clearly lactating again, so that I knew there were cubs in the sett.

Robin's apparent victory in the matter of staying at home seemed to have given her a new self-confidence. No other badger since Arwen had ever done more than offer passive resistance to Haile's threats, but one evening in March Robin surprised both Haile and me. She was on the track with Shy when suddenly he began growling and hissing from somewhere just behind me. Shy took no notice but Robin fluffed up her fur and made a rush at him. As I was sitting between them I wondered if I might find myself in the middle of trouble but she went round me and, still growling and hissing Haile slowly retreated.

Early in April I heard new cubs yikkering down at the main sett, but although I waited for a long time they were not brought up to the track. Several times during the month Frances and I heard them, and once or twice the soft purr-whickering noise that parents make to the young, but still we did not see them. The spring was very cold, as usual, and I thought that probably the sows were reluctant to let the little ones out into the east winds.

Then at the beginning of May a strange thing happened. I was sitting now, not on the track but very close to the main sett, a little behind and above the north entrance, in the hope of at last seeing something of these cubs. At half-past eight Penny came up to me and stayed for some time before trotting away up the valley. Dusk began to fall at around nine o'clock, and by nine-thirty the woods were dark. Now that the birds were silent the only sound was from the stream and the tawny owls. There was no sign of Shy, and Haile was somewhere down the valley away from the owls. Robin I had not seen for a couple of weeks.

I think that I had drifted into that state of half-dreaming one-ness with things that can happen when listening to music or in lonely places, so that the jolt was greater when I became aware of fighting noises fast approaching, howling and screeching noises of considerable ferocity. The direction seemed to be in front of me, and judging by the muted volume, across the stream and through the trees at the far side of the valley. My first thought was of Haile; was he in that part of the woods and being attacked, perhaps by some strange badger who resented his tauntings? What should I do? I had only a very small pocket-torch.

The noises very quickly grew louder and much nearer although I heard nothing cross the stream. I switched on my torch to see whatever might be seen, and to my astonishment a kind of explosion of black-and-white fur erupted from the north entrance just below my feet – fighting badgers; but which ones and how many my small light could not reveal for certain. I think that there were two,

119

but the whirl of bodies tore off into the dark woods with a diminishing sound of fury.

So the battle had not been in the distance but directly below me and underground. Questions crowded in that probably would never be answered. Who were the fighters and why? Had some invading stranger threatened the cubs, or in some other way transgressed, to be thrown out with violence? Or had Robin returned and been ejected? Had any badger been injured in the fight, and were the cubs all right?

I was not able to stay later nor to go the valley the next night, but on the following evening I was there. Both sows came up to me as usual and I was glad to see that neither appeared to have any injury; but still there were no cubs and it was 7th May, very late for a first sighting.

By May 15th, when I had arranged to go to Yorkshire for a week, there had been no change in the situation and I began to think that some disaster must have overtaken the cubs. It was at least three weeks later than the usual emergence time and six weeks since I had last heard them yikkering.

When I came home from Yorkshire I knew that the cubs had gone. It was May 23rd and no sign of them; only Penny and Shy were in the valley, mooching in the staid way of grown-up badgers and making me long more than ever for the bouncy bumptiousness of cubs. I was much preoccupied by the sad problem of what had been their fate, and could think of only two possibilities. They might have been savaged on the night of the underground fighting, or they might just possibly have been killed on the dual carriageway. We knew that they had been emerging as early as April 3rd for we had heard them, and quite early in their active infancy, cubs are taken by their elders on tours of the territory. It was on such a tour that Arwen had been overcome by cold and perhaps exhaustion (she was so tiny) and dropped behind the rest of the family. One could imagine a round of visits extending to the Forestry Commission woods and involving crossing the A3,

120

where leading badgers might just miss traffic that caught the following cubs. Still, no cub bodies were reported to me and I found none on going there myself.

However it happened, there were to be no joyful cub evenings that year, and I was more sad and disappointed than most people would understand, for the cub games had become part of my summers.

In June even the sows were away at times, probably courting, and there was no sign of Robin or any of the other yearlings. Remembering the interest and excitements of the previous summers this one seemed very subdued, with the little-used sett entrances leafed up and no welcome-party rollicking through the wood when I arrived. So it can be imagined how delighted I was to be visited on several evenings by a singularly bold and adventurous woodmouse. Often there had been run-of-the-mill woodmice who scuttered past my feet grabbing a peanut, as one taking unheard of risks in the interests of survival, but never a mouse like this one.

My usual sitting place now was by the beech hole with my feet beside an old stump under which, it transpired, my woodmouse lived accompanied by a shyer smaller mouse which I suspected to be a half-grown child.

The stump had several small deep caves among its roots and it was in one of these that I first saw Big Mouse sitting. Gently I launched a peanut to fall between my feet and the mouse, who whisked back into its refuge under the stump; but in a little over a minute it was back and had grabbed the nut and taken it inside. I flipped two more nuts and both were quickly added to the store. Nuts close by my knee were collected with great nonchalance, and in Mouse's momentary absence I had put two actually on my knee when Shy appeared from the north hole and trotted up to me. Big Mouse was just coming out of the cave, this time accompanied by Small Mouse, and was horrified to be confronted by Shy's stripy face. There was a minute explosion of dust as both mice shot back into the hole and that was the end of the mouse-party for that evening.

Lindsey is the mouse expert in our family so I consulted her, describing my visitors as carefully as I could. She knew, of course, how tiny and elegant they are, so much more beautiful than house mice, with their long tails and huge transparent ears, their pretty little faces, delicate legs and brown-silk coats, but what I had to remember was, of all things, the sizes of their behinds. Big Mouse was a female and Small Mouse a male, she told me, and explained how to tell the difference at a glance. She too thought that the small one was young of a previous litter.

During the next few evenings I was entertained by regular visits from the mice, with Small Mouse always very retiring and Big Mouse more and more adventurous. Nuts on the top of my knee were taken with complete sang-froid, and when after a day or so I put out no nuts at all Big Mouse unhesitatingly beamed-in to my jacket pocket. Since the pocket-flap was tucked inside there was no problem about diving in and finding the ultimate Aladdin's cave hoard of unlimited peanuts.

Lindsey and I were not sure how many one ought to allow a woodmouse to store away, since peanuts only approximated to a natural diet for English mice, so one evening after several raids on my pocket I pulled out the flap. Big Mouse was absolutely furious! Anyone who knows Kipling's story of *The Butterfly Who Stamped* can imagine The Woodmouse Who Flew Into A Temper. Mouse zipped backwards and forwards along the flap-seam, then sat back with hands crossed and ears and whiskers wiggling. She next slipped through the jacket opening and attacked the pocket from the inside, but the canvas was too tough. Another more determined assault on the seam proved to be no Open Sesame, so Big Mouse let off steam by rushing up my arm, across my shoulders and down the other arm before bouncing on my pocket in what was as near to a rage as ever I saw in a mouse.

At this moment Penny came padding up the bank. Instead of making a bolt for her hole as usual when badgers approached, Big Mouse whisked off my lap and took refuge under the crook of my knee, where she sat and peeped out at this enormous menace of the woods. I still think this was one of the most touching things that ever happened to me in my years with wild animals – that one might be considered by one of them a refuge in face of danger.

I realise of course that probably to the woodmouse I was only an unidentifiable Thing, too big to be viewed in focus and perhaps just handier as a bolt hole than the tree stump; but still, it pleased me to be so useful and accepted.

The next evening the mice emerged from the tree stump, delightful as ever and climbing all over me, Big Mouse even across my bare hand where she felt light and cool as she ran her shuttle service from pocket to underground store. Presently I pulled out the flap. Big Mouse stopped in her tracks and sat with folded paws as before, but this time there were no tantrums. She was working out the problem, and in a minute she had the solution. It was easy, really. What you do is, you push your nose under the flap and yourself after your nose, and then dive and you're into the pocket.

After this it made no difference whether the flap was out or in, Big Mouse just flipped into the pocket as if she'd been born and reared in one (a marsupial mouse, perhaps, brought back by Frances from Australia!) Once she even pushed my hand aside when I left it lightly on the flap to keep her out, and the next time I did this she nibbled my finger smartly.

I then tried moving a few yards away after a reasonable load of nuts had been transported to the store, but this was no good either; Big Mouse cast about like a fairy bloodhound and found me pretty well immediately, with Small Mouse in pursuit. At this point I gave up, completely outclassed by Big Mouse's ingenuity, and let her get on with it.

Frances came to the valley with me one evening and took several colour photographs, which was as well, because suddenly there were no more mouse parties and no whirling

123

whiskers in the tree stump cave. Woodmice have a short life-span, and one knows what tawny owls are – or, for that matter, badgers and foxes. But I like to think that Big Mouse and Small Mouse simply went away, perhaps to a more commodious property and further from the black-and-white neighbours.

There had been several mice in my life, including one that got entangled in my hair one night and had its page in an earlier book. After Big Mouse and Small Mouse I was visited for several harrowing nights by a woodmouse in my bedroom here at home. Unlike the old farmhouse, this house has no cracks and gaps and crannies by which mice may enter from outside, so that my night visitor must have been an escapee from one of the cats. Once inside the house, however, mice may literally go where they fancy, for all the inside doors have gaps underneath large enough to admit the stoutest woodmouse. The reason for this, I was told by the builders, is to allow room for fitted carpeting. The fact that we wanted hardwood floors with rugs made no difference to their policy on the hanging of the doors. People, they thought, ought to have fitted carpets, and if they didn't it could only be a matter of time before they regretted it; and then if the doors had been altered they would be all wrong and have to be altered again. I gave up the struggle and was stuck with the gaps, and the new mouse took full advantage of them.

I suppose it was a fairly intelligent mouse to have escaped the clutches of our cats to start with, and to scurry under the kitchen door instead of going to ground under the fridge where sooner or later fate would have overtaken it. We never did discover where its daytime base was, since all rooms were accessible, but at night its stamping ground was my bedroom – and I really do mean stamping ground. No one except my family, including Frances and especially myself, can have any idea of the noise we were bombarded with during the nights of this mouse epic.

I was a special target because in my room was a large brown paper bag of peanuts. At one time I had kept these

124

in the back porch with the wellingtons and onions and homemade wine, until suddenly it came home to me that my badger peanuts were helping to feed Maurice's and Lindsey's gerbils, to say nothing of the white mice and all the rest. I suppose they were tempting, but I wasn't going to stand for it, nor trust my grandchildren to resist temptation any more efficiently that I might have done at their ages, so I took the bag into my room.

Mouse discovered this very quickly and began making raiding attacks nightly from around 1 a.m. The noise was really astonishing. It was several nights before I realised that it could be a mouse at all, and not a couple or three rats in the wall cavity eating their way through the joists. I suppose it was thick crackly paper that made that bag, and a very furious rush was needed to scale the side and tumble in at the top, and then get out by similar tactics. I even thought about ghosts, until one night suddenly switching on my bedside light I saw the mouse, sitting up and looking at me, before casually leaving my room as if no closed door were there at all.

The family were very amused and thought it served me right for being so stingy with the peanuts. Bill offered me a mouse-trap, but after my earlier adventures with woodmice I somehow couldn't bring myself to kill this one, at least without a decent effort to catch and release it: it was a clever, audacious mouse and had already escaped one death by a mere cat's whisker.

My idea was to catch Mouse in a metal wastepaper-can, by putting a nut or two in the bottom and a sheet of cardboard with a hole in it over the top. I made steps up with boxes of writing paper. Then I lifted the main peanut bag on to my desk out of temptation's way and firmly folded down the opening.

At about one-twenty I was shaken out of deep sleep by a noise that sounded like skeletons dancing on a tin roof. My hand reached the light switch just in time to reveal Mouse bouncing up and down on my old brass letter-scales (which have engraved on them, so steady was once the pound sterling, *4 oz. 1d., 6 oz. 1½d.* This simply would not do, however furious and frustrated Mouse was at not being able to get into the bag: the whole house would be aroused.

Tottering from my bed – by now seriously short of sleep – I put a ½ lb. weight on the scales pan. It was even so impossible not to admire the prowess of this tiny creature in so easily ascending to the heights of my desk, where the usual supply of peanuts had been as instantly located as my lure in the can was rejected. I now moved the peanut bag to the top of the wardrobe; Mouse had of course departed under my closed door.

In about an hour I was aroused again, this time by a noise like hail on a dustbin lid. Ha, I thought, rushing from my bed, that must be Mouse in the wastepaper can! Indeed it had been, but a vertical take-off, skilful past belief, had fired the captive straight out again through the hole in the cardboard lid. By sliding a second sheet of card-board over the first I made the hole half as big and nearer to the centre. After an hour or so of uneasy expectant sleep the same thing happened again, with the same nerve-shattering disturbance. I roused just in time to see this fairy elephant vanishing under the door.

By this time very weary, I pushed my rug against the bottom of the door and called off the contest until another night.

At breakfast Shelley reminded me that she had said the hole was too big and too near the side, and Bill once again mentioned his mouse-trap, also adding that probably I had myself brought the mouse home from the woods in my pocket.

That night I decided the events were to take place in the passage outside my door; I would stuff the gap with my rug again and my ears with ear-plugs and not have any more sleep shattered. The hole in the cardboard was now $\frac{5}{8}$ in., central and as narrow as the under-door gap.

At two o'clock a noise of distant road-drills woke me through the ear-plugs. I tore out and peered into the can. Mouse had been there but incredibly was gone. Everyone in the house must have heard the racket, as presumably several leaps in the dark were needed before the smaller hole was successfully negotiated. There was now only one move left to me. I slid the top piece of cardboard until the slit was half an inch across. Any smaller than that and the mouse would not be able to get in, never mind out.

Restless and half-alert now, as during war-time air-raid nights, I drifted at the edge of sleep. There came a noise which I was sure was the can being flung over, despite the 2 lb. weight on the top of the cardboard. I shot out, and behold, Mouse was in the can: a cautious peep revealed it.

By now I wasn't under estimating the enemy in any way and carried the can outside, carefully shutting the front door behind me. The moment I moved aside the cardboard lid we had blast-off, and I do not exaggerate when I say that Mouse had ten inches to spare in this final spring-heeled leap to freedom.

All of us were drooping at breakfast. It seemed I had banged the door, too; I was too tired to have known. It would have been much better, Bill said, if I had used his trap: and he said Mouse was only waiting a chance to slip in again the moment anyone opened the front door, since I hadn't had the sense (or strength, I thought) to release it at the far end of the garden.

CHAPTER 17

Early in July, Penny was away for a week. There was little doing at the sett, now that the woodmice also were gone, so I spent a lot of time trying to photograph two pairs of house martins which suddenly arrived in a whirl of wings around our low eaves. We were very excited about the martins, for clearly they were looking for a building site, late in the summer though it was. To have martins under our roof would make the new house seem really established. We thought that they must have nested earlier somewhere else and for some reason had to leave and look for a new place. Our deep roof overhang was admirable for their purpose, giving shelter from rain and sun.

Luckily the ground was puddly after a few wet days, so we didn't have to make mud puddles for their building as so often we had done for the swallows at the farm. After a day or so of swooping all around us the martins settled on their sites. The first pair decided on the gable over the sitting room west window, a splendid place shaded from the south and also ideal for us as watchers, if a bit splashy for the window-glass below. But the choice of the second pair amused us and caused a tiny crisis of anxiety.

Bill had fixed up an outdoor electric bell above what had been the garage door and now was the window to Lindsey's new bedroom, so that by pressing a button in the kitchen we could call him in from the garden to meals. It was in the shape of a small dome fixed against the wall. The martins thought this absolutely ideal and fluttered close around it, settling from time to time to have a detailed look and twittering to each other, as who might say, 'My dear,

24. The seventh victim of the A3

25. The two sows brought one cub to me

26. As if I had been a member of the family

27. Raids on my pocket

28. 'Please do not ring! Martins nesting on bell'

29. F.C. Badger

30. Sprawled like dissolute Roman emperors

this is perfect! Ready-made foundations, and with a westerly outlook.'

'And it'll be an all-electric house!' Shelley said.

'No one must ring the bell,' we warned each other, dashing out every now and then to watch the start of the building, so beautifully precise and symmetrical, each small blob of mud carefully pressed into the exactly right place by beak and rounded breast.

Lindsey wrote out a mini-notice which she fixed over the bell button by the kitchen door: 'Please Do Not Ring! Martins Nesting on Bell.'

For the rest of the summer we called Bill in to his meals with a sheep bell brought back from an Austrian mountain in the farmhouse days.

I rigged up various arrangements for photographing the nests, including precarious step-ladder perches, but Sean eventually brought the matter to a fine art for me by lashing the camera to a step-ladder, fixing the flash (needed for high-speed wing movement) to a tripod and establishing me at ease in a garden chair with the cable release in one hand, a glass of cider in the other and a newspaper on my knee. This amused us all, as a skittish reaction to the dramatic bird-photographer ideal, swaying in a gale-bent pine tree at the edge of some desperate precipice.

Both broods of young were successfully brought up, but in the case of the bell-nest only because Bill rigged up a barrier to stop the cats from climbing the trellis below it. He had schemes, too, for fixing splash-boards under both nests to save the window-glass in the next summer.

About this time Haile caused me great anxiety by going missing. Often he would not return from the valley for a meal or a couple of meals, but never longer than this. After twenty-four hours I was worried and began hunting for him in all his usual haunts, but to no avail. On the third day, when there was no sign of him at breakfast, I was certain that evil had befallen him and found myself grieving for this unsociable, independent cat of the wild woods. He had often courted disaster but somehow in his charmed

129

life he had always evaded it. I wanted to go on hunting for him, but now I had laryngitis and no voice for calling. 'I'll do the calling,' Maurice offered – he was twelve – 'and you do the looking.'

So we went off together, covering the old places again and searching such few as we had not combed before. I had been meaning to direct our hunt along the bottom of Valley field, but the long grass was flowering there and Maurice had hay-fever so we went up the hill to go along the top where we had twice searched before. There is an old hedge here, full of rabbit warrens. At the top corner we paused and Maurice called, several times. Suddenly we both heard a faint mew. It was from somewhere deep under the hedge. Maurice called again, and after a minute we saw Haile's face as he came out unsteadily from under the hedge. He seemed unable to focus properly, looking hazily past us, and was very nervous, making sudden swerves back.

I decided quickly that he must have been lying up in a rabbit hole, stricken perhaps by an adder-bite or some kind of poisoning, and that this had affected his vision. He simply could not see properly. So that he should not have two of us to muddle him Maurice decided to take a short cut home and leave me to coax Haile along his familiar path, carrying him where he would allow it. He had never been a co-operative cat and it was difficult getting him home. He would not be carried for more than a few steps but he was unable to walk steadily. Perhaps because he couldn't see properly he kept making for the woods and I had to pick him up and try again.

Eventually we got home and Haile drank a lot of water and slept for a long time on his favourite chair. By late evening he was much better, seeing properly and shouting for food. The next day he was as well as ever, and we could find no mark on him. I suppose we shall never know what happened to him and the affair is filed in my mind with the many other unanswered mysteries of the valley. Certainly, whatever it may have been, it did nothing to check Haile's love of the valley; he was there the day after his recovery and on nearly every day since, as always.

Penny came back at the end of the week. It was good to be welcomed by both the sows when I took my place at the beech hole; but what surprised me was to see a third badger looking at us with some suspicion from the north entrance. It had such a broad face that there could be no doubt that it was a boar, and it was a stranger to me, not the old boar or Proudfoot or Jack and too big for Jas or Talley. Whoever he was, he didn't like the look of me and after a minute retired again underground. So Penny had brought home a boy friend? Well, splendid! It would be nice to have a father figure at the sett again after the long reign of women's lib. I wondered how he would take to Shy. Assuming that he stayed at all, would he throw her out, or take on both the females? Or, considering how big and commanding Shy had grown, would she throw him out? Or perhaps both Penny and him?

I saw him nearly every evening from that time. He never grew to accept me and always kept his distance, peering at me with deep mistrust as he prowled nearer than he felt was safe to share the peanuts. The slightest move or noise from me was enough to send him flying back to the sett, even after many weeks, although Shy and Penny were obviously unconcerned.

He was a quite splendidly handsome fellow, very black below the midline and very sleek and shiny. His frontal stripe was broad, narrowing only between the ears. He looked young and vigorous and alert. Because he seemed to have taken more than one wife and was rather regal I called him Sultan. Lindsey and Shelley queried this, knowing I had earlier played with the idea of Casanova which they thought much better, seeing that Casanova kept no females captive but sultans traditionally do; and Shy and Penny were mistresses of their own lives in every way. I tried this for a bit but found it awkward, even Lindsey's suggested shortening of Cassie which I thought a little condescending, and I returned to my second choice of

131

Sultan. The naming of animals – especially wild animals – is a serious thing and must not be done lightly. An ill-chosen name may colour one's whole view of an animal, a curious thing but it is true.

Penny I think was really Sultan's favourite, or at least I think she was the sow who loved him best. One can understand it. Shy, the former timid little thing, had become powerful and self-assured while Penny remained retiring and feminine (yes, I know I once thought she was a boar, but she was jowly when young). She also I think knew how to win her man, for at the end of an evening when some incaution of mine had sent Sultan whizzing underground, Shy would scent out and eat what she thought was the last tit-bit and then pad her way up to Valley field. I would then give Penny – who would be hanging around – a last piece of crust. Did she eat it? No! Carefully, with her head held high, she would carry it back to the sett and down into the north entrance. I like to think that she was taking it to Sultan.

In August I had news of a very unusual badger. He was one of the Forestry Commission clan and had taken to visiting a farm nearby. Jenny Tuke, who farms there, told me about him and later kept notes for me about his activities. The saga began in the spring of the previous year when Jenny brought home a family of cat and kittens and settled them in a loose-box next to the corn store. (I should here explain that Jenny's farm is a haven for the homeless. 'I've got four dogs and eighteen and a half cats,' she once said,* adding firmly, 'and there I stop.' 'Just you wait,' her brother said, 'until the next tramp comes along with his spotted handkerchief over his shoulder.') She made a hay bed in the manger for the cat family, and to keep their food out of the straw she built a 'table' of two straw bales and an old door.

After a few days she left the door open but on a hook. It was from then that she began to notice 'an incredible amount of milk being drunk by the cat family – half a

* The half was half-wild.

gallon in every twenty-four hours. All food plates also licked clean. Suspect extra cats may be coming in from the Forestry.'

Jenny decided to creep along after dark to see if the extra cats were in the loose-box. She switched on the light to find a badger who stood dazzled and blinking. The cats all looked astonished and craned their necks out of the manger for a better view. Jenny put out the light and retreated, thinking the badger would be only too glad to escape.

Ten minutes later she had another look and found the badger standing on the improvised table and polishing off the cats' food.

The next day she decided to raise the table to two bales high, which was about as much as the kittens could manage, but F.C. Badger found this no problem and came to dinner every evening.

Eventually the cats were moved to the corn store to make room for calves, and F.C. Badger followed, coming and going by way of a large cat-hole in the wall. He was seen every night by people who were going in for cow-cake, but retreated to the furthest possible corner when anyone was actually in the storeroom. He now began to cultivate a liking for flaked maize, finding no difficulty in ripping open the paper sacks. He even learned, Jenny says proudly, to unzip the sacks along the top by pulling the string, which made less trouble and mess for everyone concerned.

In October he occasionally brought a girl friend to the corn store. Smaller, with a brownish coat and extremely shy, she could be seen only by peering through the corn store window when a red heat-lamp (installed for the cats) was on.

Jenny's badger diary continues in the following spring, when she notes that F.C.B. is still coming every night. 'He has worn a little path where he comes in from the road at the back of the cowshed. His liking for cow-cake is so great that I have to ration it, but best of all he likes horse-nuts.'

A load of cow-cake containing magnesium was next delivered, in error as this was not the kind ordered. The badger and the cows were all furious, says Jenny. F.C.B. lost his temper with the whole consignment; ten sacks were ripped wide open in one night and the contents strewn about the floor. It was a relief to all when the right cake was delivered. I forgot to ask Jenny what happened to the rejected lot.

In February, Jenny notes, there were several badger fights near to the buildings, and F.C.B. came off badly with a scar on his neck and looking generally tatty. A very fierce fight broke out one evening and Jenny rushed out with a torch. The two badgers concerned stopped and gazed at the torch before disappearing into the dark, and Jenny recognised one as F.C.B.

A few evenings later she was in the corn store, and wrote, 'Hear pattering of paws in the loft overhead. Cats on bench are staring at the ceiling and say that the Canterville Ghost is upstairs. Go to investigate and find F.C. Badger up there under the eaves, behind the trunks. We peer at each other and then he turns and I see that he is going on three legs, holding up a hind one.'

And the next night! 'Bitterly cold and blowing. Relieved to see F.C.B. come in. Goes upstairs again, still on three legs. Give him extra cat food.'

Then we are into March and Jenny writes: '4th. F.C.B. has taken up residence in the loft, spending all day behind the trunks. Hope he is all right. Deliver food upstairs. All taken.'

'5th. F.C.B. still at home, sound asleep now on cats' mattress. Snoring. Get quite close, within four or five feet, without waking him. Leave food three times during day. All taken, plus dead mouse.'

'6th. F.C.B. still in, but hides behind mattress until I put food down and go away again.'

'7th. Don't actually see F.C.B. but all food goes and badger smell is still in the loft. Daren't look too hard as I don't want him to feel unsafe. Forced to muck-out loft

– it looks as if the diet is too rich for him! Provide a large tin of water as well as fish, cornflakes and milk.'

'8th. F.C.B. starts building himself a nest in the loft with hay provided (I left a large heap in the middle of the floor). Trail of hay leads under a table, round a pogostick, under the eaves and behind a cupboard and a child's (dismantled) slide. He spends the day completely hidden under hay, emerging only for meals. Second dead mouse rejected.'

'11th. F.C.B. goes out for the day, returning to the loft at night. Take opportunity to muck-out upstairs, and leave peat in lieu of dung-pits.'

'19th. Hear joyful sound of F.C. Badger pattering about on all four legs. Go up to the loft where he has stayed since the 11th and find him walking about the floor looking much better and going sound.'

Jenny's badger diary seems to have lapsed after this until August, when she resumes with, 'The Mystery of the Disappearing Tennis Balls – why he should take them to bed with him.'

We talked about it on the telephone and she told me how he *collected* these balls from their box across the loft. She found five in his hay bed during his absence, and the next day a polo ball had been added to them. Had I any idea why? Well, I hadn't, of course, but told her how the valley badgers liked to take things into their sett; to date, one dog dish, one honey jar, one blunt knife and one rubber sitting-pad. Probably F.C. Badger played ball games, since Jenny next reported, 'Polo ball has moved from one side of the loft to the other.' The cats must have thought the Canterville Ghost was having a practice knock-up.

It occurred to Jenny's nephew James that the loft was a good place to set out his model railway, and he did so, but F.C.B. coming home trundled over the lot and scattered them off the rails. James set them up again and in the morning all was scattered as before. 'It happens quite a lot,' said Jenny.

Her last note for the month says, 'F.C. Badger in all

day. Very hot in loft. Wonder if he is all right as he is lying behind the old milk-cooler, flat out with his front paws crossed. Later see him sitting with polo ball which he has now taken back to his bed.'

I went to the farm one evening to try for a photograph, but found this very difficult owing to the restricted space between the trunks and the eaves, but my Canon Camera got a picture of sorts, and I was thrilled to have seen this prodigy of badgers for myself.

Some time after this I made several more visits to Jenny's farm to see and photograph three of F.C. Badger's friends and relations who had, it seemed, discovered where he had been going and why – or maybe one might even have been F.C. himself. It was astonishing that they never noticed me, perched with my camera on a bench only three or four feet above them in the corn store. Whenever the flash fired they swung round in a 'Who did that?' manner but never looked up. Soon they settled down again, the two biggest sprawled at ease beside the torn cow-nut sacks, like dissolute Roman emperors at a banquet, and the smaller one waiting deferentially by the hooked-open door until her turn came round.

I should have liked to make more visits to the farm but Jenny's badgers were a late lot, seldom arriving before 11 p.m., so that it was well after midnight before I could get home. However careful one is it is almost impossible to garage one's car and get indoors and to bed without waking someone else already asleep, and although no one made any complaint I hadn't the heart to keep up with my disruptions. All the same, I may well risk another outbreak, after a suitably considerate interval.

CHAPTER 18

Sultan, Shy and Penny settled down for the winter together. By October they were plump and sleek as badgers should be in the autumn, although Penny remained the smallest and slimmest. Sultan never learned to trust me, confirming my previous experience that only badgers I had known and fed as cubs would accept my presence freely. I realised my wonderful fortune in having maintained friendly contact with Shy and Penny for nearly four years, enabling me to enjoy fully their family affairs including the rearing of their first cubs, and it would have been two lots of cubs now, but for disaster overtaking the second.

I watched these three adults on late autumn evenings when sometimes mist rolled down the torchbeam like smoke on the wind, or raindrops glistened, now and again catching some critical part of the beam and sparking like tiny flash-guns, or moths came floating down to brush my face. Often, misted with rain, the badgers' coats glittered frostily. On these nights there might be three different water sounds; the rush of the stream, the separate heavy drops falling from twig-ends and the patter of rain on the leaf-litter.

I thought of many things at these times, such as what had become of all the badgers I had learned to know and recognise, whether they would remember me if ever I encountered any of them again and what – if they thought in this way at all – the badgers thought about me. I wondered if these two sows were in cub again, and I hoped that they were, and would successfully rear another family for their and my delight and for the continuance of badgers in this valley.

Badgers share an unusual reproductive cycle with a few other animals, including roe deer, martens, stoats and weasels. Until the early 1930s, the badger's gestation period had puzzled biologists: it appeared to last about seven months, that is from the usual conception time about July to the usual birth month of February. But in most mammals of a similar size the gestation period is two to three months.

The first important work on this mystery was done by a German scientist named Fischer whose paper on badger embryology, published in 1931, stated that after fertilisation the egg did not become implanted in the uterus wall as usual but remained dormant and unattached. Fischer deduced, from examination of killed badgers, that implantation of the embryo usually took place soon after the winter solstice, when it would begin to grow quickly and normally. Further work done by Dr Ernest Neal shows that implantation probably occurs five months after conception, followed by an active growth period of seven to eight weeks; which means that with a breeding season from mid-July to the end of August, cubs would be born over a period from early February to the middle of March. So it is that badgers are able to mate at the most favourable time and give birth at the most favourable time, although without some form of arrested development these things would not be possible.

The year moved into the mildest winter of this century, with temperatures often above 10°C and sometimes above 15°C. In January a wren was building in a cartshed near here, celandines, stitchwort, violets and herb robert were in bloom, with innumerable daisies and a few astonished buttercups. Our cold greenhouse produced ripe tomatoes at the end of the month. In gardens there flourished mixtures of late summer and early spring flowers such as I had never seen before; cornflowers with daffodils, roses with camellias; it would have been hard to guess the time of year from either the flora or the temperature.

138

I continued my evenings in the valley, the two sows coming almost casually to my hand while Sultan prowled in the shadows and viewed the situation with unease and disapproval, though sometimes grabbing a peanut that had fallen within his orbit. Haile was often with me, amusing himself by growling and hissing at the badgers, who seldom now gratified him by taking any notice.

At the end of the winter, a year after its official approval, the first culvert under the A3 was finished, complete with its 400 yards of badger-proof fencing at each side of the road. Pat and I laid trails of tempting bait into the forbidding-looking concrete pipe and spread sanded areas for observing any tracks.

The badgers simply did not like it. On any day of the bitterly cold wet spring which succeeded that glorious winter we could walk along the fencing and see their tracks following the fence until they came to one end, where they went round it to reach the road. Sometimes the badgers went up the embankment to the culvert (the new road is raised high above its old level) where they would eat any food close to the 2 ft. diameter entrance, but they would not go more than a step or so inside. Pat and I thought about making a sortie through the culvert ourselves, if the badgers continued to avoid it. We wanted to discover whether the traffic noise and vibration were excessive, and also to lay a bait-trail and sand patches all the way through underneath both carriageways, the verges and central reservation, a distance of about two hundred feet.

There is scarcely room for an adult to crawl. We had willing offers from children but did not much like that idea. One of us would go, perhaps with a rope in case of difficulties half-way; cramp was just a possibility, and for all we knew we might even harbour hidden leanings towards claustrophobia; but we hoped that the badgers would accept the tunnel and save us the experiment.

In the end, and while I was away from home, Pat suddenly decided to do it on her own. Fitting herself out with a pair of splendid knee-caps which she uses for gardening, and old jeans, pullover, gloves and torch, she ventured into the interior. When I came home and went along to the Mill she told me, 'I've got the best news for you that you've had this year. The badgers are using the tunnel, in full force! And the traffic noise in there is scarcely noticeable.'

She had been through three times. It was a bit rough on the knees and elbows, she said, even with pads, but otherwise nothing to it.

'Supposing you'd had cramp?'

'Oh, John was around. I wasn't worried,' she said.

Naturally I borrowed her knee-caps and also made the trip to see the tracks for myself and to keep up the bait-trail. And then I wrote to the Department of the Environment to tell them the good news and ask when the work on the second culvert might begin.

After about a fortnight I had their reply which said that they were very pleased to hear that the culvert was working successfully. 'Regarding the second culvert,' the letter continued, 'we deeply regret that we are unable to construct this at the moment in the present financial climate.'

At least, I thought, with so much against them, things are better for British badgers than for the badgers of France, where they have no protection of any kind. In the Dordogne that summer I thought that I should like to see French badgers. I knew that there was a sett in woods across the fields from our friends Mike and Mariota's cottage which they had lent to Sean and his beautiful wife Saloshana and me. With Sean's better French and my atrocious resemblance of the language we asked permission of the farmer, a delightful, kindly and contented-looking man, whose woods and fields they were. He was surprised that anyone should contemplate such a rash action, considering what ferocious animals badgers were, but he had no objection if Madame insisted. We inquired further about their status and learned that naturally everyone hunted them, often poisoned them; there was a good market for

140

the skins as well as for the meat, which was considered a delicacy and served in restaurants.

I told him that the badgers in our woods ate from my hands and that the species was protected now in England. He regarded me with amazement and offered his view that I must be a very brave woman. One might have thought that I had been fraternising with man-eating tigers. (Perhaps this book may one day appear in France, to serve as an ambassador from English to French badgers?) Our farmer added a further warning concerning his fields, through which I had wandered in search of hoopoes. He had in his herd a cow which impaled women, although she only kicked men. He hadn't known about this when he bought her, and now he liked her too much to get rid of her. However, he said – my brain scrabbling somewhat inadequately to keep up with him – he would shut her up in the barn until I returned, so that I should be safe at least from her.

It was a magical evening with hoopoes still calling as I entered the wood and nightingales singing everywhere as dusk fell – and as indeed they had been doing all day. A jay perceived me as it came in to roost above me and proclaimed my presence loudly and long, so that the badgers were late in emerging (French badgers clearly have every reason for caution), but I did eventually see them, if not very clearly. I should greatly have liked to stay longer but I had, as it happened, blandly remarked to Sean and Saloshana that I should be home by half-past nine. I was not, and they came to look for me. Hoopoes do not call after dark, and we had decided on using their notes as a signal between us in case of need.

Sean can make a very good hoopoe call, good enough to converse with the bird, and presently to my dismay I heard his call approaching. It may have deceived the badgers, even at that hour, for they did not dive, but I had to reply and my un-hoopoe hooing sent them whizzing underground.

There was a moon so no torch was needed as I wriggled my way through the undergrowth and into the steep pasture.

141

To my surprise the hoopoe call came not from the field but from a deep cart-track running below it.

'Where are you?'

'In the lane. Which way were you going back?'

'The way I came – through the fields.'

'What about that cow?'

I had stumbled near enough now over rocks and hummocks to talk without shouting. 'But Monsieur Feix said he'd shut her in the barn.'

'Oh, Ma! You ought to brush up your French.' His voice came up from the stony gulf hidden below branches. 'Until half-past nine – the time you said you would be home. It's nearly ten, now. You could have been gored to death.'

This shook me a little, I admit, but I said fairly calmly I hope, 'How do I get down into the track? It looks impossible from up here.'

We hunted up and down in the dim moonlight, they in the gulf and I a little anxiously in the field with, doubtless, the impaler not far distant.

'If you try here, and jump, I'll catch you.'

It was rather splendid and exciting, leaping into the dark lane to be caught by one's son and hugged by one's much-loved daughter-in-law. I was touched by their concern.

Oh, that Dordogne holiday! Those were the days of wine and strawberries, of quiet so profound you could hear a lizard on the stones. Something splendid happened every day. There was the day when we found a rough lonely field quite crowded with stands of lizard orchids; there must have been hundreds, a marvellous sight, even in a country where wild orchids were so abundant and various that we found fourteen different species in two weeks. There was the day when, eating our crackly bread with cheese and wine in a high abandoned vineyard, a buzzard came and settled on the tip of a dwarf pine only a few feet away from us. There was the day of the kites soaring above the local rubbish-tip, where rodents must have abounded, and giving an unexpected beauty to the awful place: the red squirrel day, the swallowtail butterfly day, the green lizard

142

day; not a day without something special or rare or exciting.

For three evenings we were fascinated and puzzled by a strange sound as of distant bells, clear as prisms tinkling in the wind. On three notes, the sounds was absolutely pure, almost electronic in quality. We leaned out of the windows at the cottage and listened and guessed and wondered. The ringing always began at dusk. Was it some kind of little owl? We looked up owls in our *Birds of Europe*. There was only one which seemed at all likely and that was Tengmalm's Owl, which made 'a noise like dropping water'. Our ringing could, we thought, be likened to water dropping in a hollow place.

Roaming up the quiet lane and around two empty farmhouses we tried to locate the mysterious ringers. The sound seemed to come from everywhere but no birds floated across the moon. On the third evening we were standing on the first-floor terrace of the nearer farmhouse (the ground floor is for cattle) when Saloshana said, 'I think the sound is underneath us.'

Down the stone steps again we applied our ears to the old cracked wall that supported the terrace, and indeed it was so. With a pocket torch we discovered deep in a crevice a small toad or frog, and we saw its throat swelling as it made its fairy bell-note. Other bells replied on other notes but these ringers were too deeply hidden for us to find them.

This was a thrilling discovery, but still we didn't know what species it might be, and inevitably until we came home it was known to us as Tengmalm's Toad. Sean later tracked it down from appropriate reference books and wrote to tell me that our ringer was almost certainly the Midwife Toad, *Alytes obstetricans,* so called presumably because the male broods the bands of eggs, wrapping them around his hind legs and taking them down to the water in the evenings if the day has been dry; an arduous responsibility, but then he it is who rings the silver bells, and I hope he finds this a splendid consolation.

143

After my fortnight away I went down to the valley in hope – but not very much hope – that after the loss of cubs the spring before, this year I should have the pleasure of seeing young ones again. After all, Sultan and the two sows had been living together at the main sett for nearly a year; one might have expected cubs from one of the sows at least, but the worrying thing was that neither had shown any signs of lactation up to the time I had left for France. Perhaps there would be late cubs, I tried to reassure myself; births have been known as late as April, which would mean emergence above ground in June, the month it now was, and a sizzling hot June too, after the coldest April and May for thirty years.

Shy and Penny came to me as if I had not been away and ate from my hands, but the joy of seeing them again was sadly diminished by the obviousness that neither was in milk. For the second year in succession there would be no rollicking badger cubs in our valley. Much as I loved the two sows they were staid matrons now, at four years old, and I longed for the fun and audacity of little ones again. Sultan had grown even more retiring after my absence, seldom emerging even for cheese and peanuts until I had moved beyond the range of his short sight.

Why were there no cubs? I had no idea, and still have not. Once, several years ago, there had been two successive springs with no young ones. Dr Ernest Neal says that badgers do not always breed annually, but offers no reason. There is no overcrowding in this area, following the toll of lives on the road, and there are disused setts available. A year is a long time, and by next spring it will be two years that I shall have waited – eleven since I began year-round watching – but I know that the badger family is just one (if to me the best) of the splendours of these woods: the valley always remains, itself my reward.